TOMORROW

Create Your Future Today

Lee Ihn (Ike)

Medina, WA USA

www.ikelee.com

Printed in the United States of America

ISBN-13: 978-1986973458
ISBN-10: 198697345X

Dedicated to my family and friends who have supported me, inspired me, and believed in me.

Foreword

Do not live like today is your last day, for hopes and dreams should fill your hours. Live like someone who has many tomorrows. What drives me to constantly look forward?

When I was a child growing up in postwar South Korea in the city of Daegu, I was given a precious set of postcards from a friend. On them were beautiful pictures of the San Fernando Valley in California. In comparison to the debris that surrounded me in my city, what I saw in those postcards looked almost like paradise. I constantly looked at them to keep my dreams of living in the States strong until I could leave home. Not everyone believed I would succeed. But I knew in my heart I could create a brilliant future.

Visions of my dream Tomorrow propelled me to continually move forward. In America, with hard work, I absorbed lessons, failures and wins, new people and new places. I started from the ground up— from being an employee of a large company to CEO of my own company, eventually becoming a respected venture capitalist and corporate advisor, and now, a professor, mentor, philanthropist, and author.

I wrote *Tomorrow* to encourage those of you who are struggling to move to the next level in your lives and careers. *Tomorrow* is not something I've learned from books. Each chapter comes from my personal experience and observations over thirty years after I came from Korea with zero resources. My life has been a continual journey of transformation— each one bringing me closer to a tomorrow that started with a dream. Each day in life has a tomorrow. I hope this book will help you keep believing in your tomorrows.

CONTENTS

CHAPTER 1: WHAT CREATES MIRACLES?

"All you need in this life is ignorance and confidence, and then success is sure."
Mark Twain

"The weak can never forgive. Forgiveness is the attribute of the strong."
Mahatma Gandhi

"It is easy to hate and it is difficult to love. This is how the whole scheme of things works. All good things are difficult to achieve; and bad things are very easy to get."
Confucius

Oshin and Tampopo

Would you believe me if I told you there was a television show worth living for? In the early '80s, a phenomenon called Oshin kept most eyes in Japan glued to their TVs each morning, following the fictional life story of a girl named Oshin. From being orphaned to widowed to losing parts of her business empire in her late life, Oshin faced continual setbacks but never complained or gave up. And people in Japan didn't give up watching.

I remember reading that the death rate in Japan was down during the time *Oshin* was airing, but shot back up when the drama ended. It was noted with some concern the rate at which the residents of the retirement homes passed away after the drama ended! It appears that the residents were staying alive week after week to watch the next episode and follow the drama. The storyline was so engrossing that it kept the residents' interests peaked, their moods happy, and their stress levels low.

Ever since then I've wondered about what makes even critically ill patients able to hang on tight for their last breath. They must have something else, some human energy that is maybe not in our body but sourced externally, perhaps from their faith or endurance. People might have different theories, but I would probably call it Chi, or the superpowered energy of hope. This is tomorrow for me.

Chi is a concept familiar to many cultures and faiths—it's our lifeforce. To use a Biblical reference, it is that which God breathed into the dust to produce Adam. Chi is also the basis of acupuncture. We can increase our chi and feel full of energy, both mental and physical. And we can become unbalanced in our chi and become distressed.

I have observed for years the impact that chi can have even in the business world. Because not surprisingly, mental power is a critical element to achieving success. It's easy to blame external forces or circumstances for our failures and disappointments. But many times, we could have achieved what we wanted if we had refused to give up when faced with challenges. Let's honestly evaluate our chi and the amount of energy we invested in our goal.

In 1985, world-known director Mr. Juzo Itami created a Japanese comedy film called *Tampopo*, a dazzling, funny movie— I watched it three times! *Tampopo* was called the first "Ramen Western," a play on the term Spaghetti Western (films about the American Old West made by Italian production studios).

One scene that I still cannot stop laughing about was telling the story of a very sick mother who had just passed away in front of her three little kids. They were crying very loudly and asking for food. The dead mother all of sudden got up and unconsciously went to the kitchen, pulled rice from a container, washed it, started cooking, and fed her crying kids. Then almost immediately, after the mother saw the kids were eating, she went back to being dead!

Though *Tampopo* is a fictional story, it demonstrates a real truth—one that we also saw in the public reaction to *Oshin*. Humans can harness mysterious power when we are super focused on our goals. We can move mountains!

Motivational Focus

One way to realize your aspirations is to create a pattern that places the item of desire right in front of yourself. Years ago, when I was living in Santa Monica, I had an office in the valley to commute to every day. Then, a home in a beautiful gated community on the Avenue of the Stars in Century City (Beverly Hills) caught my eye—my dream home.

I had about a thirty-minute drive to work from Santa Monica. But after I found that house on the Avenue of the Stars, instead of driving straight to work, I drove out of my way by nearly fifty minutes each way to drive by the community. Every day I did this. Every day, out of my way, for a year. Why? I gained energy and motivation by regularly reminding myself of the house that I had my target set on.

Persistence is something that must be a constant in your world if you want to achieve dreams beyond your wildest imagination. First, listen to your gut instinct. Then, remove limited thinking. Next, you must also find a way to remind yourself daily what it is that you want with something that is real and concrete. After a year of driving by that community, I bought my dream house and drove home there every day. It definitely was a miracle for a young Korean man like me who came to America with literally nothing.

Set the Frame

In 2012, I flew to Berlin to attend a photography workshop organized by master photographer Thorsten van Overgaard. Thorsten is Danish but travels the world teaching the fine art of photography for Leica Camera.

When I arrived at the class, I had very little experience with a camera except to point and click. My classmates were all professional photographers. The kind of professionals with ten to twenty-five years of experience. Professionals who worked for well-known magazines and newspapers who wanted to learn from the master of the Leica how to improve their skills. I was out of my league.

I could not understand the technical discussions and did not understand the words used to describe the equipment or the terminology of photography. After the first day, I returned to my hotel and worried about what I would do the following day during street shooting. So I decided to just follow the master around and copy what he did. I compared his actions and shots to mine. And most importantly, I saw him patiently compose the shot and then wait. Waiting for something to happen that would complete the shot he dreamed.

My teacher called this "setting the frame." Let me explain. Most people, when they take pictures, they see what they like and snap a picture. Point and click. The basic idea is that by taking more pictures quickly, you will increase the chance of taking a good picture. But I learned from Thorsten that is not good practice in the art of photography.

The perfect picture is a combination of talent, skill, adapting to light and color, and most importantly, being patient and setting the frame. First, you must find a location. Once settled, adjust the settings of the camera so that it is optimal for the location and lighting. You have just set the frame. Then wait. Wait for the right moment when the subject and the lighting are in perfect harmony and then, only then, take the picture.

As part of a practical segment, we each went out on our own to take some pictures. I went with my friend and sat in a nice restaurant. There, I faced a long window with beautiful light. A couple came in, dressed beautifully and they sat down in front of the window. This was not yet the perfect moment, so I continued to wait. I waited a few minutes. The waitress approached. She happened to pull out a long, white menu. This was my moment! I only had one shot, and I took it. The lighting was beautiful and enhanced each individual. The subjects were lined up in a manner that the picture told a story. I had set the frame and had an amazing picture.

When we came back to class, pictures from all students were mixed and voted upon. I waited and wondered who would win. The quality of the pictures was incredible—remember these are experienced professionals. Everybody including me was surprised when my picture was voted the best among all!

I had improved my ability to take a compelling photograph even though I had never taken classes of this stature. While not understanding the technical discussions, I learned the most important lesson by observation.

What is important about a photography lesson? How does taking a great picture help me to achieve a personal goal that has nothing to do with photography? In life, you must persist until you find the perfect opportunity. If you will, you are lining yourself up for the perfect shot of achieving your goals. You are setting your frame of life. Set yourself up in the right location and then be patient. Prepare yourself with knowledge.

Believe in your ability and talent. The right moment will come along and miracles can happen to you, I promise.

CHAPTER 2: IT'S ABOUT HOW YOU CREATE YOUR TOMORROW

"There is nothing permanent except change."
Heraclitus

"To improve is to change; to be perfect is to change often."
Prime Minister Winston Churchill

"Change is the law of life. And those who look only to the past or present are certain to miss the future."
President John F. Kennedy

"Change will not come if we wait for some other person or some other time. We are the ones we've been waiting for. We are the change that we seek."
Former US President Barack Obama

Three Humble Wishes

Not too long ago I was at a beautiful event in Seattle with about one hundred people from the business investment circle. One of the hosts, a friend of mine walked onto the stage and said he would like to introduce a special person. I had no idea who he was referring to. The speaker said he wanted to recognize a businessman who had come from Asia with no resources, and when he heard this man's first investment went public years ago, he thought "he must be a lucky guy." The speaker went on that he soon heard this businessman's name again and thought, "well, he got lucky another time!" The speaker continued to hear the businessman's name a third and fourth time over the years and thought, "well those will probably be his last IPOs." The speaker admitted he was constantly underestimating this businessman though he began to follow his story more closely. Eventually they met in Silicon Valley, but he was still speechless when the businessman completed multiple M&As and a fifth and sixth IPO. Then the businessman moved to Seattle and the speaker assumed he would retire. Wrong again! The businessman had his biggest IPO ever after he "retired" in Seattle! As you've probably guessed, next the speaker asked me to stand up.

Given the meager beginnings of my story, my colleague's surprise might be considered normal. Growing up as a child in Daegu, South Korea, I only had three wishes. I yearned for a wooden desk where I could sit down to read, write, and study. I fancied my own bedroom with a soft mat to rest my head and body safely at night. And I desired a warm meal three times a day to keep my stomach filled. I had equated success in life to basic achievements.

But after my father died when I was sixteen years old, I was devastated and forced to rethink my life's plan. He was my whole world, and he was gone. For six months every day, I hiked up a mountain in Daegu that oversaw a military air force base. I watched military planes take flight and found solace in these machines that curved gracefully in the sky. The planes themselves are a realized vision of engineering and function. Here, I saw how man could push himself beyond limitations. I began to see I could make it big. More importantly, I wanted to see the real world. America was the destination I chose to fulfil my dreams.

One day I found my dream job. I realized that some employees at the LG Trading Company, one of the most prestigious and coveted companies in the Korea then, had opportunities to work overseas. That was a turning point in my life. From there, I worked hard to score a job at the company and did well as a sales representative there. It was through this experience that I learned a great deal about the international business world.

I eventually moved to the United States, and worked for a company exporting defense electronics to South Korea. Later on, I started my own company in the same field. I ran that company successfully for seven years, but all of a sudden, a recession hit the industry with the collapse of the Soviet Union and revenue fell significantly. It was my first moment of panic in the States. I took it as another challenge to prove I could move on and start another chapter in my American life.

I experienced my first failure in America. But I didn't give up and began to pursue other opportunities. A friend whom I used to work with had just started a company in the semiconductor industry, and he approached me to help with development of the Asian market. This company went public in less than three years.

In the beginning, I had zero knowledge about semiconductors, startups, or venture capital. However, I persisted and worked hard and built up my knowledge about the industry and mechanics of the business world through this experience. This was how I discovered and entered the world of startups and venture capital.

I was intrigued with the concept that one could start a business and raise capital from just having an idea, compared with the traditional models I had been exposed to where entrepreneurs usually had to stake some kind of physical property as collateral to raise funds. I realized that was the power of the American economy – companies like Amazon, Microsoft, Apple, all started this way. Ideas were the collateral of the American economy! I dived head-first into this exciting new arena. Subsequently, I was fortunately involved in several successful IPOs and M&As, where I found great wealth.

And then the dot com bubble burst suddenly. Like many others, I lost a great deal of money. It almost felt like the end of the world for me, I was devastated.

However, through this experience I unexpectedly gained perspective of what I am grateful for in life. I kept in mind that I had started my journey pursuing success and happiness, and with that I moved to Seattle with the intention to enjoy life with my family. In Seattle, I began to spend time looking at the water in Lake Washington. As I sat by the water, I started to think how I could have learned some of life's lessons more easily if I had had a mentor earlier in my career.

I decided that I wanted to help others, especially young people. I began to specialize in consulting for startups and I transformed my knowledge to become a corporate strategist and professor. Today, I regularly meet young entrepreneurs individually or at conferences and schools around the world, including in South Korea, Singapore, China, Germany, the US and UK.

Decades later, I really cannot believe what I have achieved and how far my life has come. And it happened one dream at a time. My goal now is to share the gift of thirty years of life and corporate lessons to help individuals rise beyond their own surroundings through mentorship and consulting. Yet I still find that life is full of places that I am curious to discover, new areas yet unimagined and unexplored.

Unbounded Imagination

How did I expand from having three simple aspirations to achieving a multitude of goals that have surpassed my own imagination? I would like to explore two mindsets: limited and unlimited imagination.

A mindset of limited imaginations, potentials, and achievements is constrained by its myths, its experiences, its environment. People with such a mindset are unable to envision what they can truly achieve. They do not realize their true potential and fail to identify opportunities, avoid taking risks and do not make significant progress.

I vividly remember meeting a young kid years ago selling tea on a train in India. He must have been hardly eight years old and he had a small kettle with a few earthen cups. I watched him pour a perfect cup of tea.

How did he perfect a traditional art form at the age of eight? I called him over and bought a cup of tea from him.

Like a skilled juggler in a mobile circus, he lifted the kettle and poured a long stream of the hot brew into one of the cups while holding the other cups between his tiny fingers.

When he finished, I asked for his name. After a few minutes of getting to know him, I asked him what he planned to be when he grew up.

He paused for a minute and then his face beamed. He told me his dream was to have his own tea stall on the train station platform when he grew up. I was stunned by the answer. Here is a child full of life, clearly skilled and nimble, fluent and curious and replete with future opportunities but who could not imagine a future that was much different from his own current situation that day.

Did this child lack the mental capacity or the physical ability to become something bigger than a tea vendor? Clearly not! But, his circumstances and his life experiences thus far had not allowed him to create a wildly successful mental model in his mind. With a mix of guilt and melancholy, I paid him and gave him a considerable tip. He thanked me profusely and ran off to another compartment in the train and to an uncertain, yet limited, future.

What makes a limited mindset? How is it that people are trapped, often without realizing, in states where they cannot see a much brighter future? This mindset is created by factors that are internal and external to oneself.

Internal factors include resignation to one's fate, lack of education, poverty, lack of exposure to the outside world, a stifling culture, inhibiting beliefs, repressing cultures, etc.

External factors include all the common culprits: economic adversity, political instability, class warfare, discrimination, gender bias, social inequities, etc. It is as if we form a limited mindset because we are born into families and societies that are themselves of limited minds.

How then do we escape these forces that tether us down like iron chains to immovable anchors? How do we cultivate an unlimited imagination? Consider a second example: a young man growing up in a small town in post-war Korea saw the world through the lens of the history of the place, the opportunities of the time, and the immediate success stories of his peers.

His mental model of life is colored by a damaging war that recently ended and by the wake of difficulties it left behind. The young man would desire a future that would only incrementally improve his current conditions. But when the current conditions themselves had been bleak and everybody had been struggling for years to make ends meet, even a minor improvement on those current conditions would be seen as a significant achievement.

Now, if the opportunities available to this young man were very limited, say, there were no new jobs being created in a struggling economy, then it would be very difficult for him to imagine a future working in a job that did not exist at that time. Could the son of a poor man in Daegu after the war and before the mobile phone was invented imagine working in Seoul at one of the largest mobile phone companies in the world twenty-five years later?

Or would the young man associate success with tangible examples in front of him—a neighbor who was able to buy a small house after saving money on the side for fifteen years from his meagre salary in a government office would have been considered the epitome of success for many Koreans at that time. In Daegu, Korea, myself and many of the friends I grew up with had a limited vision of a successful future, severely curtailed by our own circumstances and the environment we lived in.

How do we break free and take flight? Tomorrow is an engine of energy that powers progress towards the land of hope. There is so much I want to share from my observations working in new and different environments all over the world – starting from Daegu to Seoul, Los Angeles, Silicon Valley, Seattle (I moved 12 times in Seattle alone!) and now different parts of Asia. Perhaps that is content for another book if I can find enough time and compelling motivation. However, I want to emphasize strongly here that the most essential, fundamental condition I have found is that everything begins with the transformation of the human element.

CHAPTER 3: THE HUMAN ELEMENT

"All human actions have one or more of these seven causes: chance, nature, compulsion, habit, reason, passion, and desire."
Aristotle

"It is in the admission of ignorance and the admission of uncertainty that there is a hope for the continuous motion of human beings in some direction that doesn't get confined, permanently blocked, as it has so many times before in various periods in the history of man."
Richard Feynman

"The most common lie is that which one lies to himself; lying to others is relatively an exception."
Friedrich Nietzsche

"You can fool all the people some of the time, and some of the people all the time, but you cannot fool all the people all the time."
Abraham Lincoln

The Crucial Aspects of Character

I am often asked to identify the most important factor that I look at when interviewing startup founders pitching their ideas and seeking investments. By far, the foundation that I carefully assess in any partnership, more important than the merit of the business idea and more important than the feasibility of the technology, is the human element.

By human element, I mean the character of the founders and leaders and partners of the company seeking a relationship with me. The human element is the most difficult criterion to form an opinion on when interviewing somebody.

It is easy to understand company financial projections —they are numbers in a spreadsheet with some assumptions. It is easy to vet a business strategy—plenty of management tools and frameworks are taught in MBA school to do just that. It is also easy to assess technology— proposed technical solutions often improve on existing technologies and can never violate the principles of science. However, there is no defined rule book, no tool, no framework, no easy process that can help one definitively assess the most important factor of all, the human element.

Why is the human element so important in judging investment, partners, collaborators, employees, employers, dorm mates and life mates? There are three reasons.

First, every action in a partnership is done or influenced by a person. And people are not simple rational beings. People act, first and foremost, on their emotions, their instincts, and their beliefs. Thus, any collaboration is contingent on the non-rational decisions made by the person in charge. It does not matter if force of reason requires CEOs to make decision A—if their emotions tell them to make decision B they will almost always make decision B.

The second reason is because human beings do not change easily. We hold the wrong belief that people, including ourselves, can change their beliefs and behaviors without much effort. However, the fact is it is very difficult for people to change—our predispositions are a mix of nature and nurture. We act according to our genetic program and our upbringing and environmental influences and these are either set in stone or set in slowly forming cement. It is certainly not impossible for a person to change their character, but it is a mistake to hire somebody or befriend somebody or marry somebody in the hope that they will change down the road.

The third reason why the human element is important is because we too are humans. We have the same idiosyncrasies, same weaknesses, and same emotional drives as our partners. And unless we are somewhat aligned in character and general disposition, the partnership will turn out to be a bad marriage. And like many bad marriages, the toll of the divorce is disproportionate compared to the initial joy of the wedding.

To illustrate why the human element is so difficult to assess and yet is so important, let us look at two examples: that of Lance Armstrong who hid a character flaw for a long time and that of the Korean rapper Tablo who has been a victim of character assassination.

Fall From Grace

The Tour de France is to cycling what Harvard is to academia. It's the most prestigious of all cycle races, a grueling test of endurance, of speed, of stamina, of grit, and of will.

Lance Armstrong "won" the Tour seven times. By analogy, if Harvard produced its most prolific, most intellectual, and most financially successful graduate in one person; in the Harvard of cycling, that person would be Lance Armstrong.

He was already making a name for himself in the world of professional cycling in his early twenties winning a handful of competitions in difficult terrains around Europe. However, at the age of twenty-five, he was diagnosed with stage three (advanced) testicular cancer. The cancer had spread to his brain, his lungs, and his abdomen. His doctor thought he had no chance of survival.

But Armstrong was a fighter and went through chemotherapy, brain surgery, and tried new drugs that were just out of research labs. Within a few months after his diagnosis, to the amazement of his doctors and fans, Armstrong was declared cancer-free. He lost no time and sought to return to the world of cycling. He signed up with the US Postal race team and moved to Europe to commence training for the venerable Tour de France.

In 1999, only two years after his recovery from cancer, Armstrong went on to win the Tour. He finished seven minutes and thirty-seven seconds ahead of the second-place rider. Then Armstrong stood on the winners' podium in 2001, 2002, 2003, 2004, and 2005.

Lance Armstrong launched The Livestrong Foundation, a charitable organization founded to support people affected by cancer. Nike designed a yellow silicone bracelet for the foundation to raise money. By the end of the summer of 2004, the Livestrong wristband had become a fashion statement.

Rumors and allegations surfaced that Armstrong was using performance enhancing drugs while racing. By 2010, the U.S. Department of Justice led an investigation into these allegations. In June 2012, the US Anti-Doping Agency accused Armstrong of doping and trafficking drugs based on his blood samples and testimonies from his former teammates and other witnesses. He was stripped of his seven Tour de France titles.

In January 2013, a solemn Armstrong confessed to doping and lying about it on the Oprah Winfrey show. By the end of the show, Armstrong's reputation, which had been as solid and as tall as the mountains he so rapidly climbed, crumbled into a pile of dust.

The human element is a key part of this story. The story of Lance Armstrong is tantalizing: a man on the edge of death, beating cancer, an unwavering goal to be the best, his grueling hard work to make a comeback. This is the classic story of a hero and we want to believe it.

But was his story too good to be true? Indeed, as the old adage goes: if it is too good to be true, it probably is. Often the most dangerous people believe their own lies and it would be impossible to even catch them in a lie detector test. We must carefully reflect on the people we partner throughout our careers because faulty character can ruin even the best opportunity.

Much Ado About a Stanford Degree

The Canadian-Korean rapper Daniel Lee, who goes by the artist name Tablo, was a prodigious child. From an early age, he demonstrated exemplary skills playing the piano and violin. At age seventeen, he was already writing lyrics that were becoming popular pop songs sung by Korean stars.

His parents saw the talent in their young son and convinced him to enroll at Stanford, hoping, as many Asian immigrant parents do, that he would become a doctor or a lawyer. Daniel's interest in music and especially hip hop bloomed at Stanford. In 2001, he met two Korean rappers and formed the band Epik High and started experimenting with his own genre of Koran pop. At the same time, his academic performance kept apace.

Tablo graduated from Stanford in 2002 after only three and a half years as a student with two degrees—a Bachelor's degree in English literature and a Master's degree in creative writing. Little did he know then that breezing through Stanford would turn into a windstorm later in his life.

Epik High defied the norms and traditions of a me-too music culture and addressed unspoken topics such as racism and class warfare. By their fourth album, they were breaking up the top music charts in Korea and being featured on magazine covers. They were also banned on certain TV channels due to the nature of their songs, and caused the Ministry of Culture and Tourism in South Korea to restrict the buying age of their CDs to nineteen. Tablo and his rapper group had arrived.

Nobody believes the trope that every successful rock star marries a famous movie star, right? Wrong! In 2009, Tablo married the gorgeous Korean actress Kang Hye-jung. The following year, the couple welcomed a cute baby girl and the tabloids sent paparazzi to photograph the family even in the maternity ward.

Oh, one more thing—a few years earlier, Tablo published a book titled *Pieces of You* that sold 50,000 copies in its first week of release, topping the bestseller's list in Korea! Tablo seemed to have it all: handsome looks, gorgeous wife, cutest child, powerful art, bestselling book, legions of fans, Western-Eastern citizenship, and Stanford degrees.

Let's pause here for a moment. Was it too perfect a picture? The clues all seem to point that way, right? But let's see.

In May 2010, a Korean online group going by the name "TaJinYo" created a forum titled "We Request the Truth from Tablo." The anonymous group did not believe the near perfect story of Tablo. TaJinYo asked a simple question: how is it that Tablo finished two degrees from Stanford in only three and a half years. In a country where a Master's degree alone takes two full years to complete, that question appeared to be a very legitimate one.

Tablo initially did not respond to TaJinYo's allegations. Let's pause again. This is a vital clue about the dynamics of the human psyche. Tablo's reaction was to the commotion regarding his degree, not to the validity of the degree. In the first place, Tablo had not used his degree to establish authority or dominance. After all, a degree in literature is not very material to his current profession of producing rap music, right?

Not so for many people in Korea. After the tabloids reported the existence of TaJinYo, membership of the website swelled to 200,000! The anti-Tablo movement sent hundreds of emails to Stanford asking the university to verify Tablo's credentials.

Stanford's registrar, Thomas Black, issued a formal statement affirming that Tablo was indeed an alumnus of good standing from

Stanford and that "any suggestion, speculations, or innuendos to the contrary are patently false."

At this point, one would think that the masses would be satisfied. Reasonably, Stanford, a prestigious university, would not lie about Tablo's degree and ruin its reputation for a single student, especially when the records could be revealed so easily. Unfortunately, the attention did not cease.

TaJinYo members took that to believe that Tablo must have appropriated the identity of another actual Stanford graduate going by the same name. As bad luck would have it, another Dan Lee did indeed graduate from Stanford that same year. The detractors started contacting him too!

As matters got worse, Tablo's wife started receiving calls berating her for marrying a liar. His mom was harassed with callers leaving threatening messages, and his brother was fired from his job. And Tablo himself received death threats.

There is a second force of the human element at work here which is crowd psychology, sometimes called "herd behavior" that impact large groups of people and often leads to riots. A conspiracy theory horde can manufacture any lie and believe in it. The conspiracy theorists were turning into any celebrity's worst nightmare: a violent mob!

Tablo did everything he could to combat this growing wave of hate: he published his Stanford transcript, explained his family history, released his passport to the press, and sought out co-alumni to verify his story. Nothing worked.

Tablo avoided the public. He feared for his life and for his family's. In a matter of months, a simple lie had turned him from Korea's poster boy to Korea's most wanted. And then a challenge came. The producer of an investigative Korean show called *PD Note*, like America's 60 Minutes, challenged Tablo to travel to Stanford and request a transcript of his degree in person and on camera. Tablo took up the challenge.

In August 2010, followed by a Korean camera crew, Tablo walked the manicured lawns at Stanford, met with people who remembered him as a student, and visited the registrar's office. He presented his passport and diploma to the registrar and made a request for his transcript while the camera was rolling.

The registrar accessed the database while being filmed and printed the transcript then and there. He then compared it line by line with the one that Tablo had in his possession and on camera confirmed the exact match of the two documents. That footage was turned into two *PD Note* episodes and aired on national TV to a rapt Korea gathered in front of their TV as if watching the first man's landing on the moon.

Soon after, the government prosecutors who were investigating Tablo confirmed his claim and attested to the fact that he was indeed a Stanford graduate. They further demanded that Naver, the largest community site in Korea hosting the online forum, divulge the identities of Tablo's online attackers. The lead agitator turned out to be an American-based businessman.

What does this story mean? What kind of human elements are at play here? For Tablo, he was telling the truth, he had the proof to back it up, but yet, the crowd was not happy until they had reached a point where government officials stepped in to help resolve the issue.

Besides these two examples, I've seen many similar cases that were started by someone jealous of a person doing well, trying to harm them and enjoying watching them fall down. This has even happened to myself. In one case, an individual sent letters to my contact points advising them not to deal with me because of fake drama that the person fabricated. I ended up losing some contacts from that event. There are many haters out there who will do something just to hurt you or enjoy watching you going down the hill.

The Most Elusive Criterion

I chose the stories of Lance Armstrong and Tablo to demonstrate that it is sometimes very hard to detect or dispel a lie, even when the lie is in front of the whole world and carried over a long period of time. Lies, like other character flaws, can be absolutely damaging. It is damaging to the person lying and the person being lied about.

How then do we judge people's character when we hardly know them? How do we avoid falling into such traps and avoid associating with such people? The answer is to trust your gut instincts.

If you encounter somebody and there is a certain reservation in you about that person, then do not make them a partner you would need to depend on. You may not be able to quite put your finger on why you have this reservation. You may not even be able to articulate the reasons to yourself. You may not be able to fully understand why you have such feelings towards the person.

The reason is this: a gut instinct is *not* just a random feeling. A gut instinct has evolved in our body to signal the brain if there is danger. Your subconscious mind is collating many pieces of internalized data: minute body expressions, choice of words, forced tones, evaluations of gain and loss, personality types, everything you know is subconsciously being rendered and the result is a gut feeling.

But we also know we have to be careful of bias and stereotypes, which I discussed in my last book, *Wonder*. So how can we tell the difference between an unfair bias and an instinct that is accurate? Your gut instinct will be as strong as the body of data it can compare against. Using the gut instinct—an elemental part of being human—can be improved by being aware of your surroundings and taking in all the detail around you. Increase your curiosity in the world around you, and become involved in areas that challenge and fascinate you, these steps will help to grow your instinct into a strong tool. If your world is limited, your gut instinct will be limited.

If your gut is warning you, pay close attention. I have never, and I want to emphasize *never* here, been successful partnering with somebody with whom I had an initial bad feeling. I have always been disappointed when I went against my gut feelings and formed a relationship.

On the other hand, whenever I had good feelings about somebody, that person more often than not turns out to be reliable. Whether it is in marriage or in business, listen to your deep-down instincts. As Gandalf the wise wizard advised, "If in doubt, Meriadoc, always follow your nose."

Experiential Transformation

The Experiential Transformation is the need to change our experiences of everything that our senses capture. We need to expose ourselves to various sights, sounds, touches, tastes, and smells. It is only through the voluntary perceiving of a new experience can we expand our exposure to life.

Taste is another great sensory experience that we should act on. Try new foods, new cuisines, and new restaurants. Do not be afraid of trying food from a completely different culture even if it looks strange. I love watching the show on CNN by Anthony Bourdain. He is always discovering new tastes and through the tastes discovering new people, new cultures, and so much more in life.

Increasing the number of experiential events you have will ultimately increase knowledge inside of you. This will help strengthen your gut instinct. Expanding my sensory experiences helps to generate an incredible pool of data that my gut instinct and rational mind can and will use to make better decisions.

CHAPTER 4: PICK YOURSELF UP

"I have not failed 10,000 times. I have not failed once. I have succeeded in proving that those 10,000 ways will not work. When I have eliminated the ways that will not work, I will find the way that will work."
Thomas Edison

"Only those who dare to fail greatly can ever achieve greatly."
Robert F. Kennedy

"Success is not final, failure is not fatal: it is the courage to continue that counts."
Winston Churchill

"The only real mistake is the one from which we learn nothing."
Henry Ford

Accepting Failure as Inevitable

Think about what it takes to compete in the Olympics. Let us take swimming as an example. The typical swimming athlete trains for six hours a day every day of the week, for years, before the event when they will compete. It is a grueling exercise —hours spent in the pool, lifting weights, running on the treadmill, listening to the coach's instructions and practicing again and again the minutest details of the swim. Add to that the strict food regimen to be followed religiously—a swimmer eats to build stamina and body leanness to glide in the water and to propel the body rapidly.

Physical training is only one part of the complete drill —psychological preparedness to get ready for the Olympics is equally daunting. Getting the mind ready for years for an event that would last only a few minutes is no easy task. Now, imagine the day of the Olympic event: a hundred-meter freestyle race in front of a cheering crowd of thousands with millions more watching live throughout the world.

The stakes are high—the winner not only goes home with a gold medal but will live forever with honor, respect, and a place in history. Business and marketing deals will follow—reputation and richness are guaranteed. Now, imagine if after a tense competition with world-class athletes and all these years of intense training, our athlete misses first place by a fraction of a second!

In the summer of 1992 in Barcelona, Derek Redmond, a 400-metre record holder, took position at the starting line of the Olympics 400m semi-final race. He was at the peak of his athletic career and was one of the favourites for the Olympic gold medal, having won multiple medals in numerous championships and games. He had had a tumultuous athletic career, interrupted many times by difficult injuries, but his incredible perserverance brought him back on the race track again and again. This time around in Barcelona, despite having had eight operations in four years, he had won the first two rounds a without any difficulty.

Midway into the race, however, a most unforeseen situation happened. He tore his hamstring and fell to the ground. In his own words, "the pain was intense. I hobbled about 50m until I was at the 200m mark. Then I realized it was all over. I looked round and saw that everyone else had crossed the finishing line. But I don't like to give up at anything – not even an argument, as my wife will tell you – and I decided I was going to finish that race if it was the last race I ever did."

Determined to finish the race, he hobbled to the finish line with the help of his father, with the support and cheer of a 65,000-strong crowd in the stadium. Since then, this incident has been voted one of the Olympics' most inspirational moments by US network NBC, it was even referenced by Barack Obama in a presidential speech. Redmond could no longer compete in distance runs, but he did not give up his athletic life, switching to play professional basketball. Today, he is an acclaimed motivational speaker and trainer and shares his inspiring athletic journey and experience with audiences around the world.

Imagine the disappointment, frustration, letdown and anger that would naturally swell in a human's heart. Is this failure? A loss? A washout? Or is this an opportunity to derive a lesson that can prepare the athlete for something better in the future? How can an athlete even overcome the apparent failure?

Sometimes we are taken down roads we never expected and do not want. When that happens, we have defining choices to face. We can persevere, like Redmond did, or we can give-up our dreams. Isn't it the same case for failures in businesses?

Loss Aversion

In order to pick ourselves up to continue the humble journey, it is important to understand the significance of loss and our natural resistance to loss. The pain we feel from losses outweigh our pleasure from equivalent gains. The brains of human beings are wired to weigh losses heavier than gains. Imagine the following situation: say you overheard your boss suggesting to his boss to offer you a pay raise of $500 per month. How would you feel? Happy and pleased, I would suspect.

Now, imagine the same conversation you overhear, where your boss is now suggesting that your salary be cut by $500 per month. How would you feel? If you are like most people, you would feel disappointed and angry and not just sad. Your negative feelings in response to the cut are stronger than your positive feelings about the raise.

What does this mean? It means that the pain we feel from failure is experienced more strongly than the pleasure from an equivalent success. It is not rational, but this is the way our brains work. This is the concept of loss aversion. When we face setbacks and failures, we may be irrationally magnifying the losses that occur. In this light, how do we keep moving forward despite our innate response to avoid and prevent loss? How do we move to the next level of our journey if there are feelings of insecurity about the future? Darwin has an answer.

Failure is Darwinian

The English philosopher and biologist Herbert Spencer coined the term "survival of the fittest" after reading Charles Darwin's *On the Origin of Species*. Spencer had already been developing ideas that societies and cultures evolve, an idea that would later be called "Social Darwinism."

Spencer's ideas have been extensively critiqued. He is often considered one of the greatest intellectuals of the nineteenth century. I do not offer to take up Spencer's ideas here; however, I would like to propose that we view failures as events that make us fitter and increase our chances of survival.

A failure is a mismatch between an attempt at doing something and the best outcome for the target audience. Let us understand this definition. Imagine a group of people whose individual and collective states could be improved if they were to experience a new concept. I am using the term concept a bit loosely here and a new concept could mean a new idea, a new product, a new service, etc.

If the new concept succeeds in advancing the state of the people, then there is coherence between the new concept and the intended group of people. The new concept achieves a best outcome for its audience. Take the Apple iPhone as an example. The iPhone as a concept improves the state of its consumers by a significant margin.

It allows them to stay connected and achieve things that they could not do before. Because of this high coherence between the concept and the best outcome, the iPhone is a great success. On the other hand, if the concept does not improve the state of the targeted audience, i.e., the best outcome cannot be achieved, then that concept is a failure. In other words, a failure is one attempt that could not survive because it was not the fittest.

Now, per the above definition, a failure is only a concept that is out of sync with the best outcome for an intended audience. The end goal in this picture is not to create a concept for the concept's sake but rather to improve the state of the people. The failure just happened to be one mismatch in an attempt at doing that. Seen this way, a failure is not an end in itself. It is rather a lesson on what not to do when we re-attempt the next concept to achieve the best outcome for the intended audience.

Our aim in life is not to try once, fail and then give up. Rather, our aim in life should be to try often, fail fast, and never give up.

This is how humanity, whether biological or cultural, has always evolved. Our environments are too complex for us to achieve success at every turn with absolute certainty. We cannot design failsafe concepts all the time. We are bound to create systems that do not achieve best outcomes. Instead of regarding these incidences as catastrophic, we need to regard them as data points in our broader attempt at achieving best outcomes. We pick up after failures and try again.

In my work, there have been many occasions where I did not succeed in my attempts to make deals with different companies and investors. As disappointing as these incidents were to me, they allowed me to understand what did not work, who not to approach in the company, how to improve my pitch, how to rephrase my plans, how to frame my proposals.

In the years to come, I brought many other deals to these same companies and have been successful in getting them to sign agreements with me. I used the incidents of failure to retune my future approaches, which enabled many future successes.

Winston Churchill once said, "success consists of going from failure to failure without loss of enthusiasm." There is so much truth in this statement. It is our ability to bounce back after a failure and be ready to fail again that guarantees success. Seeing failure in a different light, as an opportunity for future success is liberating. It allows us to chase success without fear. And it allows us to enjoy life without worry.

Limited Control on Our Fates

Take a minute and look back at your life. You will realize that you are where you are at today because a set of distinct events have happened over the course of your life. You went to a certain elementary school where a certain teacher illuminated your imagination, you met a certain person who became your best friend, you were admitted to a certain university, you lived in a certain part of town, you married a certain person whom you fell in love with, you got a certain job with a certain company, etc.

Now, look back at some of the less pleasant memories. Maybe you did not get through an interview or were rejected by a certain college. Maybe you broke up with a loved one or lost money on an important financial investment. Maybe a project went in a different direction or you were betrayed by a friend or business partner. If any of these events happened to you, maybe you lost hope. Perhaps you felt that the timing was never right for you.

Life is not a continuous and smooth stream. It is rather like a river, calm at some places, rushing at others, cascading occasionally and filling lakes every now and then. Now ask yourself how much control you had at each of these twists and turns that have defined your life.

Life is so complex that it is hard for us to understand every turn—what often appears as a failure could be a step towards a greater success and vice versa. We try our best in life. Yet, more often than not we have limited control over the most important events we encounter and that truly make us "us." Let us look at life situations from another angle.

Consider the life story of Jan Koum, the founder of the runaway messaging mobile application success, WhatsApp. In 1992, Jan left his native Ukraine and immigrated to Mountain View with his mother and grandmother. They were escaping a difficult political and anti-Semitic environment.

Once in the US, they needed the help of the local government in renting a two-bedroom apartment. The family lived on food stamps and Jan's mother worked as a babysitter to make ends meet. Jan would not have an easy life in his early years. He worked as a cleaner at a grocery store. He enrolled at the San Jose State University only to drop out.

He joined Yahoo! where he met Brian Acton and the two developed a close friendship. Both Jan and Brian applied to Facebook and were rejected. The friends launched WhatsApp in 2009. Jan insisted on a solution that does not store users' messages; he was too wary of Big Brother spying on the common citizen in his native Ukraine.

The app offered free international texting and it quickly took off worldwide. By 2013, with a staff of only fifty employees, WhatsApp grew to 200 million users. Mark Zuckerberg developed a personal interest in the company. He called Jan Koum to his house and discussed the future of the company.

In 2014, Sequoia Capital, which invested in WhatsApp, brokered a deal where Facebook acquired the company for $19 billion. Jan signed the deal in front of the Community Center where he used to stand in line for food stamps.

What would have happened if Jan had not "failed" a few times in his life? What if his family had not feared government surveillance in Ukraine? What if he had not dropped out of university in San Jose? What if Yahoo! was not failing and Jan had a stimulating desk job at the company? What if Facebook had not rejected him?

We will never have answers to these questions. All we can say is this: a series of apparent failures ultimately led to a huge success for Jan Koum.

Likewise, in our own lives we should not be overly worried when we face setbacks. Like the old saying goes: when one door closes, another opens.

Emotional Transformation

Once we accept that we have limited control of events, how do we break free from loss aversion and accept that failure is a test to try again? A mental transformation that breaks us free from a limited mindset is an Emotional Transformation. Why is it important to take this approach to our own emotions?

It is because unless we believe in ourselves, in our own abilities, in our own potentials, in our own competencies, nobody else will. We need to develop a sense of self-esteem, self-respect, self-regard, courage, and dignity that fire up all that we can then do.

Hence, the first transformation is one that is not pivoted on well-thought out reasons but rather on a belief deep in our heart that mankind, which includes us, is indeed infinitely capable.

We need to retune our emotions to believe in what is beyond our immediate visible scope. We need to first and foremost believe in ourselves, and to be able to trust in our own abilities not just as an individual with limited means but as part of a human race that has transformed this planet. We must convince ourselves that irrespective of the limitations that the world around us places on us, we can be much more than that.

We have to suspend limited sensorial logic and believe in our abilities in an almost spiritual way, to believe in the unseen and the imagined. We must dream. We have to have faith in the greater good that man in general, and we in particular can achieve. We must develop a passion deep inside our hearts for success even though we may not have one clue as to how to achieve that success. In my first book, *Wonder*, I call this lighting the fire in one's heart.

CHAPTER 5: THE STREET IS MY R&D CENTER

"How much can you know about yourself if you've never been in a fight?"
Quote from the movie 'Fight Club'

"I think the most important thing about coaching is that you have to have a sense of confidence about what you're doing. You have to be a salesman, and you have to get your players, particularly your leaders, to believe in what you're trying to accomplish on the basketball floor."
Phil Jackson

"If we put before the mind's eye the ordinary schoolroom, with its rows of ugly desks placed in geometrical order, crowded together so that there shall be as little moving room as possible, desks almost all of the same size, with just space enough to hold books, pencils and paper, and add a table, some chairs, the bare walls, and possibly a few pictures, we can reconstruct the only educational activity that can possibly go on in such a place. It is all made 'for listening'"
John Dewey, "The School and Society"

"If I had learned education, I would not have had time to learn anything else."
Cornelius Vanderbilt

Street Smart Navigating

When I arrived in Los Angeles in the early '80s, there were not many job opportunities were available to me other than blue-collar work. But that was not what I had come to America for. So, I began months of diligent observation and research to find out what the leading industry was at that point in time. From there, I settled on the booming but very highly controlled defense industry as my primary target.

How brave I was! A young Asian immigrant who came to America with no relevant background, trying to get into an exceptionally restricted circle like the defense industry. I was insane! In fact, I'd heard the word INSANE many times but I didn't care because as a non-native English speaker I didn't understand the meaning of it anyway. Even if I did, I would have done it anyway. Without being insane, there is nothing you can achieve. You have to be crazy enough to believe in what you want to achieve!

Several times over, I was rejected. But my dream was important to me and nothing would stop me. I kept knocking on doors until finally someone gave me a chance, someone recognized that I was motivated and hungry to prove myself to do job right. I was hired as a sales representative to the Korean market to sell communications components and various high technology defense equipment. I didn't disappoint the CEO who trusted in me and gave me the opportunity. Within a short period of time, by working hard around the clock and bringing in profitable business, I became the best sales representative of the company.

How did I break into this industry without any relevant background and without any formal training? How was I able to get a job, that in hindsight, would seem impossible to fathom? I was successful because I approached things in a different way.

Being book smart is to understand life from theories and well-defined models. Being book smart is to have a firm grasp on the foundations of what makes things work the way they do. Being book smart is to understand how the sciences and economics influence the world.

But life does not follow a straight path, life is not a clear chart that follows a grand theory. How can we improve upon book knowledge and be prepared for curve balls that come at us both professionally and personally?

To be street smart is to have both the experience and the knowledge to effectively deal with situations at hand. It is a repository of information that one gathers over years by actually facing and tackling life situations. It is learning from practice and learning put in practice. It is the intuition to do the right thing by trusting one's guts.

Street smart is an ability to read people's emotions, understand nuances of behaviors, and pick up on body language. Street smart is being comfortable with subjective complexity. Street smart is understanding how emotions influence the world. A truly smart leader is both street smart and book smart.

The Hardwood Warrior

Phil Jackson grew up a religious boy in rural Montana in the 1940s. Jackson was naturally tall as a boy and was good at basketball. In high school he led his team to win two state titles and the University of North Dakota recruited him on a basketball scholarship, where he led his team to the NCAA Final Four twice. In 1967, the New York Knicks drafted Jackson, giving birth to his long-celebrated career in the NBA that continues till today.

During the 1969 season he had to sit out on the games due to surgery. He decided to do something he had never done: publish a book. So, he started gathering observations in a format that could be consumed by a broader audience, and spent his time documenting the Knicks games in his first publication, *Take It All*. He. He would go on to write seven more widely acclaimed books.

In 1980, Phil Jackson retired as a basketball player and started his coaching career. He spent several years coaching teams in the basketball minor league in the USA and in the regional league in Puerto Rico. He applied for jobs in the NBA but was repeatedly turned down. Finally, in 1987 the Chicago Bulls hired him as an assistant coach. It was also there he developed a magical mentor-mentee chemistry with a young Michael Jordan.

Jackson was promoted to head coach in 1987 and he implemented a set of revolutionary coaching techniques. He introduced his players to tai chi, made them practice yoga, instructed them to meditate, led them to play in the dark and in silence, and had them read self-help books. Borrowing from Buddhism and Native American teachings, he emphasized a philosophy of "mindfulness", and prepared his players to be strong in mind, strong in spirit, as well as strong in body.

In 1999, Jackson was hired to coach the other great team in the NBA and the fierce competitors of the Chicago Bulls—the Los Angeles Lakers.

He brought his techniques with him and got equally interesting players like Kobe Bryant and Shaquille O'Neal to play as a strong unified team.

In his illustrious coaching career, Jackson accumulated a total of 11 NBA championship wins, and holds the record for the coach with the most number of championship wins in the history of basketball. In 2007, Jackson was inducted into the Basketball Hall of Fame and is widely considered as one of the greatest NBA coaches of all time. Jackson documented his team management philosophy in several books, including in the 1995 bestseller *Sacred Hoops: Spiritual Lessons of a Hardwood Warrior.*

His books have become very popular among leaders in the business world and some are mandatory readings in MBA programs in the top American business schools. Jackson himself never took a formal business management class and certainly has no MBA. He learned all he knows on the hardwood floor of the basketball court. Jackson is street smart.

The School Dropouts

There are countless successful people who, like Phil Jackson, went to little-known universities. They have no doctorates or formal business trainings. They work very closely with the common citizens, interacting often. They quote religious figures and historical leaders; Phil Jackson quotes Buddha and Hopi wisdoms.

I, for one, believe that is important to round sound theoretical knowledge with a strong practical understanding garnered through actual experience. I understand the importance of being book smart, and yet I have an equal, if not greater, appreciation of those who are also street smart.

In Pink Floyd's 1979 masterpiece "Another Brick in The Wall," the British group sings, "We don't need no education / We don't need no thought control / No dark sarcasm in the classroom / Teachers leave them kids alone / Hey! Teachers! Leave them kids alone." Since then the song was the de facto national anthem for all those, from truant kids to new age leftists to radical school reformers, who believe that a structured school system enslaves the brain and kills ambition and innovation.

Reformers complain about everything about the school system: that the classroom with its "desks placed in geometrical order" is designed only for listening and not for debating, that the lessons taught do not reflect real life challenges, that the students are being taught local skills whereas the economy is global, etc.

One popular reform coalition called the Partnership for 21st Century Skills (P21), whose membership organizations include Adobe Systems, Apple, Dell, Hewlett-Packard, Microsoft, and Verizon, argues that "every aspect of our education system must be aligned to prepare citizens with the twenty-first century skills they need to compete."

The arguments that I often hear from such groups are along the following lines: "just look around and you will find many leaders who became successful only after they dropped out of school!" I, for one, believe that those who call for an overhaul of the education system make some valid arguments. However, I do not believe that a complete tear down and reconstruction of our school programs propose better education solutions.

While we look at several great leaders who became successful after they dropped out of school, this is not an advocacy for school reforms. I am using these examples to demonstrate that great success can be achieved even without formal higher education. I am emphasizing that being street smart is an important ingredient to success. I also want to note that many of these leaders are great learners and read more books than academics. Hence, they also demonstrate book smartness.

The most famous school dropout is Bill Gates who did not complete his degree at Harvard to go on and launch Microsoft and change the world. But Bill Gates is an avid learner. He is friends with smart people like Nathan Myhrvold, seeks counsel from mentors like Warren Buffet, attends conferences like the Sun Valley Conference hosted by Microsoft's co-founder Paul Allen, listens to TED Talks and reads voraciously. Bill Gates maintains a page on his foundation's website where he recommends and reviews books. To Gates, being street smart is learning through all these channels.

Li Ka Shing, the billionaire owner of Hutchison Whampoa, dropped out of school at age fifteen. Now, he runs one of the world's largest conglomerates with operations in over fifty countries. The company employs over two hundred thousand people in industries ranging from telecommunications to energy to infrastructure to hotels. Mr. Shing, who started his career selling wrist watches, said about his humble beginnings, "The first year, I didn't have much capital so I did everything myself. I had to keep my overhead low by learning everything about running a business, from accounting to fixing the gears of my equipment. I really started from scratch."

Sir Richard Branson, the colorful billionaire founder of the Virgin Group, which controls over four hundred companies, dropped out of school at age sixteen. Sir Branson has dyslexia and had poor academic performance as a student, and on his last day at school, his headmaster told him he would either end up in prison or become a millionaire. He would go on to found his first successful company before he was eighteen and bought his private island at age twenty-four. Among his many achievements, he worked with Nelson Mandela to launch a small group of global leaders, known as The Elders, to solve very complex problems, such as poverty, AIDS and climate change, that impact people around the world.

Larry Ellison once remarked that he had "all the disadvantages required for success." He was born to an unwed mother who gave him up for adoption. His cold adoptive father told him that he would amount to nothing. He dropped out of college twice—once from the University of Illinois at Urbana-Champaign and then from the University of Chicago. Ellison would go on to found Oracle and attain wide fame and success. His personal net worth is over fifty billion dollars. He has signed The Giving Pledge started by Bill Gates and Warren Buffet committing to give part of his wealth to charity.

Henry Ford was born on a farm in abject poverty. He was never formally schooled. From an early age, he taught himself to fix watches and used the watches as textbooks to learn the rudiments of machine design. He worked as a mechanic and learned how to repair steam engines. He worked in barns and small shops across the country trying to build "horseless carriages." This hands-on learning experience would prepare Ford to launch his eponymous company that would change the world. The curator of the Henry Ford museum noted, "He (Ford) often took jobs because he didn't know how to do them, and they were opportunities to learn. It's a very gutsy way to learn."

Other famous school dropouts include Steve Jobs, Ray Kroc, Walt Disney, Michael Dell and Mark Zuckerberg. Very successful personalities who never went to school include Andrew Carnegie, Mary Kay, Mayer Rothschild, Frank Lloyd Wright, and Dhirubhai Ambani.

My aim again in highlighting these examples is not to suggest that a formal education is a bad thing. Indeed, I am a strong believer in a solid educational foundation. I am rather explaining that, despite not having any education or despite not having colorful advanced degrees, many of our business heroes were very successful.

The way they achieved this success is in developing an ability to learn from their situations, learn on their feet or learn from the street. Being street smart is an important ingredient to being a great and successful leader.

Eight Tips from the Street

My students like the practical lessons that I have learned from my years of working in the VC world. They appreciate the examples that I can bring to life, the learning I derived from failures and the joys I gained from success.

They prefer hearing about personal stories as case studies rather than memorizing complex economics formulas. They can relate to and remember recounted emotions more easily than memorize the logic of calculated reason. So, what have I learned from the street? What is it that I teach my class?

Here are eight tips that I have picked up over my life, not from books, but from the University of Life; these tips were published in *Singapore's Straits Times*:

1. *Focus on the customer*: What does the customer want and need to make their interaction with you a memorable one? As I made the case in my first book, customer experience is the one factor that rules them all to ensure your business is on a path to success.

2. *Target the small but significant*: Most big product successes are not grand inventions, but small yet significant tweaks to existing products.

3. *Soak up advice*: Meet people, network and learn as much as you can from them; then, think clearly how that advice can be relevant to your business.

4. *Practice your pitch and practice again*: Learn to tell your story in ten seconds or less.

5. *Have a plan*: Do your market research thoroughly, know your potential customers inside out, and build a plan with short-term and long-term projections. I often advise my students to build a ten-year plan with yearly milestones and each yearly plan with monthly sub-milestones; then on a daily basis determine if you are making progress towards the milestone in front of you.

6. *Trust your instincts*: If something does not feel right, it probably is not. This is especially true when choosing a business partner.

7. *Avoid talk of failure*: Do not believe in the credo "failure is an option." You cannot start a venture assuming it will fail. If you have a plan B before you even start your plan A, you are already thinking about failure.

8. *Enjoy discouragement*: Knockbacks are inevitable. Entrepreneurship and pursuing your professional life is about believing in yourself and constantly pushing forward and not getting discouraged easily. Discouragement has been my main source of motivation.

CHAPTER 6: STOP LOOKING FOR A CRYSTAL BOWL

"Real knowledge is to know the extent of one's ignorance."
Confucius

"The learning and knowledge that we have, is, at the most, but little compared with that of which we are ignorant."
Plato

"I was bold in the pursuit of knowledge, never fearing to follow truth and reason to whatever results they led, and bearding every authority which stood in their way."
Thomas Jefferson

"Knowledge has to be improved, challenged, and increased constantly, or it vanishes."
Peter Drucker

Save Your Old Newspapers

I settled in to my seat for the long flight home back to the U.S. and pulled out a lengthy contract I needed to review. I spent a couple hours underlining sections and taking notes, and I eventually got so tired I took nap. Before I knew it, we had landed at the Seattle airport, and I didn't realize till I got home that I had forgotten all about the contract. I searched everywhere and couldn't find it. Luckily, I found a copy of the contract in my email but I had to redo all my work. What a waste of time!

I forgot all about this day until till five years later I found the paper contract sticking out of a Korean business magazine I had apparently had with me on the plane. It was tucked next to an article titled "Top 10 Promising Companies." I got curious where these companies were at now and started to read the article. I knew pretty much every company there — but I couldn't believe it — at least four were out of business, one was barely surviving, and a couple more had CEOs that had gone to jail!

How is it that expert analysts and journalists had raved about these companies and now these companies are non-existent? I have never forgotten this lesson. Now I like to routinely look back at old business articles and see the connections that only hindsight can bring. I encourage you to try this experiment in your sector. Maybe you can avoid the pitfalls other failing companies have experienced. And certainly, you will learn to think more critically about current business predictions and trends.

This is my recommendation – find an old magazine, newspaper or periodical you have and read it. How much of the content do you find relevant now? Put one or two on your shelf (don't collect everything!) and make an effort to look back at it every year. Even if you skim it briefly, it will make you think a lot about our world and how the way we think, work and live changes so rapidly.

When you sift through a current periodical, ask yourself how many of these companies will still be around in five years. Or, ask yourself whether your own company will still exist in a few years from now! Do you believe in the conventional, current knowledge that uplifts these companies? If so, they should all be doing great for many years to come. But we know statistically, many of them will go bust and five to ten years from now.

Building upon the foundation of the most powerful invention of modern history, the internet, humankind is creating more and more incredible technological breakthroughs today. Concepts and prototypes are being tested for driverless cars, quantum computing, machine learning, genetic forecasting, among other world-changing innovations. Our lifestyles are shifting much more rapidly than before. Some of these technologies and businesses may prevail in ten years from now, while others may be swept aside by the winds of change. Perhaps some time in the future, you will look back at today's knowledge, or lack thereof, with some amusement.

A Scientific Study Lasting 1400 Years and Counting

Sir Karl Popper, a great philosopher of science in the twentieth century argued that scientific theories, and human knowledge generally, are generated by the creative imagination of people trying to solve problems that arise within their specific historical and cultural contexts.

In his book *All Life is Problem Solving*, Popper explains that scientific theories progress not through proofs but through falsification. The conjecture that is hardest to falsify survives as a tentative theory and is the best "fit" to solve the problem at hand. But times change and theories no longer fit. And the cycle then repeats itself. It is through this process that knowledge expands.

Popper's theory is remarkable for one more element—it does not assume that knowledge is finite. Per this theory, since solving one problem generates many more problems, knowledge is always growing and is indeed infinite.

From a street-smart perspective, let's take a look at this. After you have worked hard to achieve something, does the process leave you unchanged? No. Your knowledge has expanded. This is another reason to immerse yourself in the Experiential Transformation. You are literally generating possible solutions that can be applied to achieving success.

Let us look at how humanity's understanding of the theory of gravity changed over the centuries. In fourth century BC, Aristotle remarked that motion must exist only if there is a cause. He contended that heavy objects move towards the center of the universe while lighter objects, such as fire, rise up to the heavens.

In the sixth century AD, the Indian astronomer and mathematician Brahmagupta suggested that the earth was spherical and that it attracted objects towards it. In the ninth century AD, the Arab mathematicians Al Hamdani and Al Biruni wrote, "we say that the earth on all its sides is the same; all people on the earth stand upright, and all heavy things fall down to the earth by a law of nature." In the seventeenth century AD, Galileo found that all objects accelerated equally while falling.

Then in 1687, Sir Isaac Newton published *Principia*, which hypothesized the inverse-square law of gravitation. Newton's theory of gravity achieved tremendous success as it accurately explained the motions of the planets in our solar system.

However, in the nineteenth century discrepancies in calculation of planetary movements using Newton's law were surfacing. In 1915, history's other great physicist Albert Einstein published the general theory of relativity and explained these discrepancies. The theory of gravity, which was being thought of as early as the fourth century BC by Aristotle, would take its current form only in the twentieth century with Einstein!

As you can see, the theory of gravity evolved over centuries with one scientist building upon the work of a previous scientist in a process that mimics that of Darwinian evolution—weak theories were discarded while strong theories were improved.

Popper's theory here makes the case that each idea was valuable for its context and time. As the idea was refuted and as it faced new challenges, new ideas had to be sought. By that count, even Einstein's theory may be falsified one day and the replacing theory will be more elegant and more robust at explaining gravity. If scientific knowledge is not finite, what about our own general knowledge?

The Magic of Infinity

In many cultures in the East, the master starts the training of their students by teaching them that they know almost nothing and that they will never attain full knowledge.

Buddha is known to have said, "The eye sees many things, yet can never truly see itself / The mind thinks many things, yet can never truly think itself."

I once asked a Middle Eastern friend of mine why is it that some chapters in the Koran start with words that nobody knows the meaning of—chapter two, for example, starts with the mysterious word formed by the letters A, L, and M. And he told me that being mysterious is a way for God to teach humanity that despite all the knowledge we have, there are certain things that we will never know. This approach to knowledge, that knowledge is infinite, is very healthy. Let us see why.

First, knowing that knowledge is infinite grounds us in humility. We know that we know only a drop of all knowledge out of the vast ocean out there. Realizing that fact will remove any ounce of arrogance from our hearts. We will not think, like I did at thirty years old, that we know everything there is to know.

Second, appreciating that knowledge is infinite opens up vistas of curiosity for us. We realize that there is so much more to learn and know. We do not take everything for granted except with a view that we can improve upon it. This can be anything—from a process to run a company to an idea in our mind to a political system we have come to like.

Progress is always possible. The term "Medici Effect" refers to the explosion of innovation that happens when knowledge from many disciplines is allowed to grow and freely mix. We need to create our very own "Medici Effect" where we remain open to knowledge from all sources and let them mix to combine into a depth of intellectual acumen and sublime character.

Third, we will not take hard and fast stances on our ideas and actions if we grasp that knowledge is indeed infinite. We will be open to criticisms, refutations, and feedback for these can help us refine our own positions. We remain flexible. We listen. And if the message received makes sense, we change our own position. This is a key leadership trait.

Fourth, we live within our contexts and our time. Our knowledge is formulated based on our own experiences and our milieus. We understand that others with different experiences and different milieus will arrive at a different set of knowledge. And so, we do not impose our understanding on others who may live in a different context and time. We appreciate other people's positions. These different milieus could be people from another country or culture. Similarly, we approach ideas from another time with caution noting that mindsets were different then.

And lastly, we appreciate the complexity of the world in which we live. No idea and no scientific theory are baked in cement. Life is complex and understanding of life is complex. It takes centuries for us to get some ideas right and even then they will change. Appreciating that the world is more than a black and white tableau opens our minds to its complexities. This fact, as simple as it is, is difficult to grasp for most people.

True leaders are humble. They never claim that they know everything. They listen, they learn, and they adapt. They know deep inside that knowledge is infinite and they only know a little bit of what there is to know. They, however, remain curious and always seek to expand their own knowledge.

Let us look back and take a closer look at the idea of a limited imagination and unlimited imagination from Chapter 2. How can we make the transfer between a limited mindset to unlimited? Mathematically, you don't have to. *The knowledge already exists.*

When I say knowledge is infinite, this is exactly what I mean. In a mathematical sense, there is always room for more knowledge. No matter how much knowledge we gather, there will always be an infinite amount of knowledge out there. The only thing required to have an unlimited imagination is to believe that you can!

CHAPTER 7: SINGING WITH A NEW YORK CABBIE

"Was I always going to be here? No I was not. I was going to be homeless at one time, a taxi driver, truck driver, or any kind of job that would get me a crust of bread. You never know what's going to happen."
Morgan Freeman

"I think that anybody's craft is fascinating. A taxi driver talking about taxi driving is going to be very, very interesting."
James Lipton, American writer, lyricist, actor

A Profession With Two Directions

Driving a taxi is one of the most grueling professions out there. A taxi driver is locked in a vehicle that is locked in a grid of roadways locked in a city for hours on end. The workplace consists of a steel car on a tarry road surrounded by gray cement buildings. Add the constant din of honks and street noise, the pollution from exhaust pipes, and the stress of traffic and one gets a nightmarish work environment.

The job entails being constantly alert: alert to other cars, road debris and potholes, traffic enforcement police looking to dole out tickets, and potential customers standing by the sides of the streets. Taxi drivers have to deal with all types of clients in a hurry to get somewhere: the businessman who is late to a meeting, the mother with a crying infant on her way to a doctor's appointment, the family returning from a vacation trip with oversized luggage, and the late-night partygoer who is inebriated and rowdy.

The job has its dangers too. We often caution about not getting in a car with a stranger; a taxi driver is always picking up a stranger on a curb and letting that unknown person sit behind him with the driver in a more vulnerable position.

Through their interaction with people from all walks of life, they gather a very broad perspective on pertinent matters. They are living mobile data miners. They develop a keen sense of judgment and can quickly understand people and situations.

In my travels around the world, be it in Shanghai, New York, Paris, London, or Seoul, I often engage taxi drivers in conversations. Taxi drivers, who spend their days and nights on the street, are literally street smart. They are always out there in the world meeting with the whole cross section of humanity during their shifts.

I often initiate conversations with them to learn what they have learned, to understand a new city from a mind roving that city, to get a perspective from the street. There is an excitement that comes with the serendipity of meeting a person for a first time and establishing a very human bond with them for the short time that we interact. I have often found the excitement of getting to know my taxi drivers exhilarating. I have made some good friends this way and have really enjoyed my rides.

More often than not, the taxi drivers can accurately tell me, within a few minutes of talking, about myself. They start by asking me, "May I ask what you do for a living?" Then I ask them to guess. In most cases, they tell me that I must be involved in some kind of financial business or in the academic field.

There is an uncanny similarity among taxi drivers all over the world. They are generally men who are somewhat confident, somewhat risk takers and always hard working. They often have responsibilities to fulfill, such as a family with kids to raise.

Taxi driving is a job where demand rarely goes down; hence it is a good profession for first-time job seekers. It is a bit of an irony that those who know a city best are often its foreign-born taxi drivers. Taxi drivers also often have an immigrant work ethic and will take on the job that more established citizens with the advantage of local education, local language, and local connections may refuse.

The common thread that runs through taxi drivers all around the world attests to the common bond of humanity that binds all of us. We may live in different cities and speak different languages, but our aspirations as well as challenges are often very similar.

After decades of conversing with taxi drivers, I can categorize them in two groups: short-term cabbies and long-term cabbies. In the former category, the drivers are in the profession with a mindset that they will one day graduate into another less demanding job.

In the latter category, the drivers have found a way to enjoy the profession and they believe they will retire as cabbies. The lessons from both of these categories are applicable to other demanding professions. When we find ourselves in a difficult situation at work, we have two options to resolve the problem. We can work with the intent of finding a better opportunity and consider the current job a short-term stepping-stone. Or we can find higher meaning and satisfaction in that difficult job, making it a pleasant long-term opportunity. Let us explore.

Seeking A Better Opportunity

The short-term cabbies see taxi driving as a difficult job but a decent source of income. It does not take much to become a taxi driver: a driving license, a clean driving record, and some experience.

There are companies who hold the medallions and rent out the cars to aspiring drivers. Hence, taxi driving is a profession that a person with little former experience can get into. The returns can also be attractive. All it takes to make a taxi driver's day is to pick up one customer who needs a long ride.

While any typical city has many taxi drivers, the demand is always there. The fare rate is usually fixed and the money is collected right after the ride. I have often encountered drivers who are in the profession because they need a source of immediate cash. They may be students who are driving part-time or recent immigrants with a family or even highly skilled workers laid-off from a more professional job. These drivers are using taxi driving as a short-term stop on their way to a more satisfying and less demanding career.

In my conversations with this type of driver, I am often asked what advice I have for them so that they can find a better opportunity. Before answering, I always ask them whether they would listen to me and act on my advice. I get a smile back followed by a "certainly!"

My advice for the taxi drivers all around the world has always been the same. I ask them to go walk through a few conventions held in the city. It does not matter if there is a convention on agriculture or space exploration or handicrafts; I ask them to just go there and walk the halls. This advice surprises them at first.

Then I elaborate. Conventions are a concentration of the best that a certain industry can offer. It is a focal point where the best in that industry sends their best employees to set up their best displays and make their best pitch of their best products. And it is a place where a diversity of ideas from one industry all comes together. Walking a convention hall is as fascinating as walking through a live encyclopedia on an industry.

Conventions always capture attendees' imagination. They are a fertile ground for new ideas. If you are not sure what to do next in your career, just attend a few conventions and let yourself be amazed by the displays. Put your mind to work and let the inspiration flow in. My short-term taxi drivers love the unconventional idea! And it is one of the first steps in helping them to see the possibilities of an unlimited imagination to fuel their career aspirations.

Once I attended a formal dinner at a very prominent person's place in Singapore. His house was located on the beautiful coast of Sentosa. The dinner ended late and I needed to grab a cab back to my hotel in the city.

Another guest dropped me at a depot and I waited for a cab there. I never knew that finding a cab late at night in that part of Sentosa could be difficult. I waited for nearly thirty minutes before the first cab came by to drop a passenger. I rushed to the taxi only to realize that the driver was not planning another ride that night. He looked visibly tired and he told me that he was closing for the night. His wife was pregnant and he needed to rush home. Since I waited for so long to see the first taxi, I was worried that I was standing at a bad spot. I asked the taxi driver to drop me at another better spot to find another taxi on his way home. He looked at me, realized my challenge and agreed.

As I sat down in the back of the cab, I asked the driver about his wife. He looked at me in the rear-view mirror, thought for a moment, and then asked, "Are you Mr. Lee?"

I was stunned! The driver was certainly a stranger to me; how did he know me? I answered affirmatively. The driver's face lit up and the annoyed frown turned into a smile. He had read my interview in the papers this morning and saw my picture.

The journalist had asked me about entrepreneur tips and my driver turned out to be an aspiring entrepreneur. It also turned out that both he and his wife had taken business courses in London. His wife was pregnant and he needed an immediate job to make money and so he was driving a cab while he found a more permanent job. He started talking to me about the newspaper article and soon we were chatting as if we were long lost friends.

Without informing me, my Sentosa driver made a U-turn and told me that he would drop me at my hotel. I insisted that he needed to be home with his pregnant wife. It was in vain. He felt obliged to accommodate me; he could not leave me waiting for another cab on the curb in the middle of the night.

I gave him a lot of advice and we had a wonderful conversation along the way. When he dropped me, he came out of the car to shake my hand and refused to take his fare. I, of course, insisted and would not let him go without getting paid. We exchanged phone numbers and hugged. We both learned from each other and made a new friend that night.

Sinatra-Singing Cabbie in Manhattan

I once hailed a cab in New York. The driver was an older gentleman close in age to me. He was very pleasant and welcomed me in with a broad smile. As I sat in the car, I realized that he was listening to Frank Sinatra on a magnetic tape. And as the car started off, the driver started humming the tunes along with Sinatra.

I was surprised that first, a New York taxi driver could be in such a good mood and that second, he was listening to songs on magnetic tape. The tape was worn out through the constant friction of the moving parts and the music and sounds were not high fidelity. I lost no time and started a conversation with him. I quickly learned that this had been his prized possession for many years. It turned out that the tape brought much joy to this driver. I told him that Frank Sinatra, on this tape, sounded like the singer Johnny Mathis, who has a different, slower singing style. We started laughing. We entered into a nostalgic discussion about the music icon. Before we both knew it, we were singing along with Sinatra all the way from South New York to Times Square. By the time the driver dropped me in the middle of Manhattan we were both holding our bellies and laughing!

I learned that my Sinatra-singing cabbie had been driving cabs for a very long time. The long-term cabbies are of a very different breed. They are often older men from the local population who work fewer hours. They have been in the profession for a long time. They usually own the cars they drive. They tackle the challenges of driving around with a more relaxed attitude. They are not darting around and have a generally sunny disposition. They are not looking to change their profession. How can people who are in such a demanding profession relax into a cruising pace? How have they been able to ignore all the stress and even find the work pleasant?

In my conversations with these long-term cabbies, I realized that they have taken to view the profession very differently from the short-term cabbies. They cite the many benefits of the job: they work on their own schedule, they have no boss to report to, they can take a break in-between rides whenever they want, they are never in one place, they are always discovering new places in the city, and they meet a huge diversity of people. These drivers found meaning in their profession.

In fact, they cannot comprehend how a person can sit and work behind a desk in a windowless office every day for years on end. The long-term cabbies have been able to replace in their mind the challenges of the job with the higher benefits of the job. And beyond that they found satisfaction and actualization in the profession.

At one point or another in your career, you will feel that the profession you are in is very demanding. You will have two options: work through that job with a mindset of finding a better opportunity or re-pivot the profession in your mind, finding its less salient benefits.

When you find yourself in a position that requires such a decision, be sure to consider all that you know. Like a cabbie, you should have a destination in mind. Look at your map. Check in with your gut instinct—is this the right time for a move? Or are you anxious to get rid of uncomfortable feelings?

Through observation and research, find different solutions. Set yourself a schedule and explore opportunities in non-traditional ways like visiting conventions or use the time to find a higher meaning to the job. Uncover and realize benefits to continue with an employer.

Remember the business degree-holder cabbie in Sentosa or the Sinatra-singing cabbie in New Jersey—both of them will end their professional career with satisfaction and success! Recall that life is not a straight path. Remember that the decision you make will be with the best intention and knowledge that you have. Believe that the best will happen, but if it does not work out the way that you want, do not lose hope. Keep your eyes focused on your biggest goal, and always move towards your dreams.

Professional Transformation

After a careful assessment of your career choices and assessing which decision is right for you at the time, it is important to know that job change is inevitable. In the twenty-first century economy, staying in the same job is unwise. Fortunes of companies go up and down all the time and one job is never secure. Staying at one job too long is in effect a calcification of one's opportunities.

In the present-day economy, you need to change your professional career every few years. Force yourself to discover new opportunities by shifting jobs, changing companies, changing roles within the same company, taking on new projects, developing new skill sets, going back to school, learning something new, etc.

We need Professional Transformations in our lives. A professional shift is the only way to expose yourself to more work-related opportunities. There is a simple test that I use to know when I am ready to shift professions: when I feel too comfortable in my current profession, I know it is time to do something else. When it is the right time, be prepared to move on to the next opportunity.

I have constantly pushed myself to study and learn new fields, new technologies, and new tools. Throughout my career, I have always tried new jobs. I never let myself get too comfortable with one profession. I worked in the international trading industry in Seoul, in the semiconductor and electronics defense fields in Southern California, as an investor in start-ups in Silicon Valley, and as a strategic advisor to corporations and startups in Seattle.

It is said that Omar the Great would switch to eating olive oil when he started enjoying butter and switch to butter when he started enjoying olive oil. He never allowed himself to become the prisoner of either butter or olive oil! Likewise, do not allow yourself to become the prisoner of a cushy job.

A professional transformation is exciting but can be difficult. It will often require you to be open to different types of transformations at the same time. You may need to move geographically and be prepared for experiential transformations that challenge you both mentally and physically. Rationally, you may wonder if the change is right, but still maintain a deeply held belief that you will achieve your goals. It is hard work, but I believe you can do it!

CHAPTER 8: QUEST TO THE INNER CIRCLE

"Sometimes, idealistic people are put off by the whole business of networking as something tainted by flattery and the pursuit of selfish advantage. But virtue in obscurity is rewarded only in Heaven. To succeed in this world, you have to be known to people."
Sonia Sotomayor, Associate Justice, Supreme Court of the USA

"You can make more friends in two months by becoming interested in other people than you can in two years by trying to get other people interested in you."
Dale Carnegie

"If you want to go fast, go alone. If you want to go far, go with others."
African proverb

"To furnish pleasure, happiness and health to all its members. Pecuniary profit is not its object."
Articles of Incorporation of the Los Altos Golf & Country Club, Oct 29 1923

Los Altos Golf & Country Club

The Los Altos Golf & Country Club, located in the heart of Silicon Valley, is an oasis of greenery and fresh air that offers to its select members an almost therapeutic escape from the daily pressure of the high-tech industry.

With majestic views of surrounding California golden hills and the expansive landscape of its professionally designed eighteen-hole golf course, the club has a feel of liberating openness. The rich and ornamental Spanish design of the clubhouse adds to the grandeur of the place. And at an astounding half a million-dollar membership fee, the club is one of the most exclusive private social associations in the world.

Membership is, of course, by invitation only and requires a sponsorship by four existing members. The club, being a gathering place of the titans and aspiring titans of Silicon Valley, unofficially concentrates the power of Silicon Valley. It is said that more deals get done over brunch at the club on weekends than in boardrooms during office hours on weekdays.

The Los Altos Golf & Country Club is a vital node of the Silicon Valley high-tech network. When I relocated to Silicon Valley, I quickly realized that being part of this club is a catalyst to success. I had been a member of private clubs in Southern California previously and I knew very well that a tightknit influential social group can accelerate success. Now that I was going to work in Silicon Valley, I resolved that I needed to become a member of the exclusive Los Altos Golf & Country Club. Being a member of this club became my new goal and as I always do, I immediately paid full focus and tried to find the way to achieve my goal in short period of time.

In those days Tracy O'Rourke, the CEO of Silicon Valley pioneer Varian Associates, was the board president of the club. Varian Associates was located on Hanson Way in the valley and my incubation center happened to be right across the street from Mr. O'Rourke's office.

Mr. O'Rourke had by then already had a very successful career. He was a turnaround legend. Varian Associates was one of the first high-tech companies in Silicon Valley. The company was founded by two brothers in 1948 to manufacture the "klystron," a device to amplify electromagnetic waves at microwave frequencies. The company had a celebrated history. It was one of the few postwar technology companies around which the whole Silicon Valley crystallized.

Hewlett Packard, the other Silicon Valley pioneer, was located a few blocks from Varian Associates. In the 1950s, the US government contracted Varian Associates to build the fuse for the atomic bomb, effectively trusting the company and its engineers with the design, engineering, and manufacturing of the most sensitive component on the most destructive bomb man ever made. However, by the late 1990s, Varian Associates was struggling and Mr. O'Rourke was brought in to reinvent the company.

To become a member of the Los Altos Golf & Country Club, an aspiring candidate needed to secure the sponsorship of a primary member and the approval of three other existing members.

This is no easy task. I decided that I needed to influence Mr. O'Rourke himself. If I could convince this turnaround rock star at the helm of a technology pioneer, it would be easy for me to get the approval of three other existing members. But, I had little chance to get a meeting with a busy CEO who had never met me.

I knew I had to get the word out to him that I wanted to become a member of the club. The task was daunting for a newcomer in town. I had few connections and little influence in the Valley at the time. However, I was determined to make a break in my new city and I believed in myself. So, I set out to find a way to get a meeting with Mr. O'Rourke.

I worked my then fledgling network and reached out to any contact who may in some way be connected to Mr. O'Rourke. These were the days before LinkedIn and when a network was organized as business cards on a Rolodex or in a shoebox.

If we are all only six degrees of separation away from Kevin Bacon, in Silicon Valley we are all only three degrees of separation away from any power player.

I used that fact to my advantage and called friends and then friends of friends. With painstaking effort, I slowly but surely managed to find a track connecting me to Mr. O'Rourke. I discovered a mutual friend that I asked to be my sponsor and write a letter of introduction to Mr. O'Rourke. Then I wrote my own letter and filled out a membership application to the club and pushed it through that track to Mr. O'Rourke. Once I knew my missive had reached his desk, I could only pray that he would read it and act on it. So, I waited.

Some two weeks later I was sitting at my desk when out of the blue I received a call—Mr. O'Rourke wanted to see me in his office within fifteen minutes! I dropped whatever I was doing that day, grabbed a coat, and rushed to the Varian Associates' headquarters across the street.

How to Build Your Own Network

There were several factors at work here that helped me to meet Mr. O'Rourke. My success was not something that happened overnight. It was built layer by layer. When you are building a community, this takes time. Networking is an oft-used word that has become cliché in many quarters. MBA students take full courses to learn it, marketing and sales folks claim it is their only job, and executives swear by it. The fact of the matter is that many people talk about networking but few do it right. Few truly benefit from the advantages of networking.

First, let us define networking. Networking is the establishing and maintaining of a relationship with a select group of relevant people whom we can rely on to further our goals and who, in turn, can rely on us to further their own goals. Note, the many qualifiers here: networking is both establishing and maintaining relationships—this means that it is an ongoing process. Relationships can be social, professional, philanthropic, etc. The people in the network need to be both selected and relevant. And most importantly, they need to derive benefits by being connected to us as much as we derive benefits by being connected to them. If done right, networking does not simply multiply our reach. Rather, our reach is raised to the power of the people we know. A network provides an exponential increase in our impact and efficiency. In other words, a network can also be defined as what we know raised to the power of who we know.

My detractors often wonder how I established a strong network starting with nothing. Below are guidelines I have discovered during my career that have enabled me to create and maintain efficient networks that have greatly improved my chances of success.

Step #1: Actively seek out gathering places

The Los Altos Golf & Country Club is a physical gathering place that, as I said above, concentrates the power of Silicon Valley. It is the ultimate modern watering hole for the successful and influential. Physical gathering places include conferences, social associations, meet-ups, non-profit events, sports venues, local joints, popular restaurants, etc. Virtual gathering places include online blogs, social networking groups, mailing lists, online forums, bulletin boards, WhatsApp groups, etc. A gathering place effectively acts as an efficient way to connect people with like-minded objectives. To derive the benefit of a network, you need to be at the gathering place.

Once you have identified the network you want to be part of, you need to locate its gathering place and then actively seek to be part of it. As I have demonstrated above, this is often not trivial but unless you are welcome at the gathering place, you will be an outsider of the network.

Identify the watering hole of your desired network and then ascertain a means to be part of it. And, once you are part of it, you need to be actively present there.

Step #2: Do your homework first

Before becoming a member of the Los Altos Golf & Country Club, I researched the club extensively. I learned its history, understood its programs, and toured its grounds. Then I mapped out the influential members of the club.

Once I had identified Mr. O'Rourke as the President of the club's board of directors, I found any connection in my existing network to him. I learned about him, his past, his successes, and his plans at Varian Associates. I read all newspaper clippings about him, went over his interviews and asked others about him. I did my homework first and when the opportunity came to meet with Mr. O'Rourke, I was fully prepared. I felt I was meeting somebody I knew well even though it was the first time I was shaking his hands.

It is important to do your homework on the network you want to belong to for another reason. Networking consumes time, energy, and resources with often indirect and uncertain benefits. You do not want to be wasting energy on networks that consume you and yet have little probability of improving your own success. So, do your homework, be informed, be choosy, and be prepared.

Step #3: Know what you bring to the table

A network link is a two-way connection. Remember that at all time. It does not matter if the person you are trying to link to happens to be the President of the United States. If you desire that he take you seriously, you need to demonstrate that you can bring value to the relationship.

This is often very hard, especially when you are trying to network with people who are position-wise, job-wise, or wealth-wise higher than you. However, consider a number of things that you can bring to the table:

your own experiences, your ideas and observations, your background, your history, your cultures and beliefs, your feedback on the other party's interests, your own contacts, etc.

Contribute your good demeanor, joke often (no silly jokes), and make the other party laugh. Connect on something that you both have in common: kids' school, local neighborhood, social causes, etc. You always have something to add. It is also important to remember that, irrespective of a person's position in life, they are still a human being just like you.

Sometimes we create these oversized images of dignitaries and celebrities. However, everybody is very similar deep inside. Rich and influential people also have insecurities, weaknesses, idiosyncrasies, and worries like the rest of us.

They also have a need to intellectually connect with others and may be wanting to talk to you more than you want to talk to them. Do not be intimidated by who they are. Rather connect with them at a human level.

A cautious note here: I have found that people, in an attempt to force a connection, go out of their way to please the other party. They sometimes lie and often overcommit as to what they are willing to do. Such people tell you what you want to hear when you meet them. They commit to everything you want them to. It is easy to commit and forget or fail to deliver. Try to establish a connection but do not force one. Bring to the table only what you can really deliver. One of my evergreen wisdoms is, "It is always better to under-commit and over-deliver rather than over-commit and under-deliver!"

Step #4: Be prepared and rehearse

"Luck is what happens when preparation meets opportunity," is an old quote often and likely mistakenly attributed to the Roman philosopher Seneca. There is much truth in the adage—preparation is key to a successful meeting.

Preparation means taking time well before the meeting to think through what we may expect out of the meeting, who will be at the meeting, what topics may be discussed, what are the expected outcomes of the meeting, what roles the attendees could play, what would influence them, what are your desired take-always from the meeting, action items, etc.

Before you set out to network, take time to think the meeting through. The worst mistake you can make is to go to a networking event unprepared as that may have the negative effect of damaging your credibility and position in the network. It takes time often to get a meeting and you do not want to lose the one opportunity to make a bond.

Once prepared, rehearse! Rehearse the talk you need to give, the point you need to make, the idea you may need to explain. "Practice makes perfect" is the other old adage that is very true if you would like to achieve maximum success.

Step #5: Tell stories

Storytelling is as old as humanity itself. In fact, it is a core aspect of our behavior that has allowed people to live together in groups, to communicate, to recount history, to remember battles fought and won, and to build beliefs, myths, and legends.

In some ways, storytelling is instinctive to human nature. Storytelling is the stitching together of words to convey an idea, a meme, in a manner that is interesting and that one can remember. Note, by storytelling here I do not mean embellishing facts or lying. Rather, I mean framing your message in a narrative that is impactful and easy to digest.

When you meet people in your network, do not attempt to get their initial attention by laying out data. Often times, we want to quote metrics and numbers from the start of a meeting. This is common among technology company founders and engineers.

In my experience jumping to data is an approach that rarely works. Always start your meeting with a pleasantry or a joke if you can pull it off. Then frame your message in a narrative that the other parties can both emotionally and rationally connect to. Connect to your listeners at a personal level. Ask them about themselves. Show interest in their children, their families, and their causes. Then use these hints and craft your own narrative weaving your message into the conversation.

Step #6: Be yourself

When we meet someone who we need, there is a tendency for us to exaggerate our statements to impress the other party. Think for a minute about the dynamics during an interview. The person seeking the job is always emphasizing how good they are at everything. We tend to do the same thing when we are networking with others, especially people who are higher in grade than us.

In my experience, this is a mistake. It does not help but rather hurts us when we overstate our experiences, magnify our accomplishments, and extend the truth. How can that hurt us? It hurts us because the other party is at least as intelligent as we are. Successful leaders can very easily detect when someone is telling the truth or when someone is embellishing facts to get noticed. To be successful at networking, always be who you are. Listen attentively, think before answering and making a point, remain humble and respectful, quote data only when you know they are factual, ask genuine questions, do not be shy to say you do not know, and change your own positions if the other party makes a more convincing argument.

To be yourself, you need to know yourself well and know yourself truly. As we explored in my first book, *Wonder*, this is often harder said than done. We are all biased towards our own ideas and behaviors. To be taken seriously, you need to be able to genuinely understand your abilities and limitations and then accordingly contribute to others. We are all born with things that are valuable. Find those in you and leverage them to build your network.

Step #7: It takes more than one meeting

Networking is more art than engineering. It requires a good deal of interaction and a lot of dedication without a clear expected outcome. Often times, it costs a lot of money and time too. You cannot approach networking as a computer code where if you input ten hours in three meetings with eight people then you expect two job offers as output.

While many of us know that this is not the case, we often do the mistake of approaching people with this sort of formulaic expectation in mind. Networking is all about people connecting. The aim and goal of networking is simply to make connection. Do not measure your network's value by the outcome of every meeting or by expecting a benefit from everybody you meet.

Let's say, through hard work and careful planning, you finally meet an individual who can help you achieve your goal. Of course, it is very exciting to finally meet this person. This person might have unique insight to a problem, or they might have a contact at a company you are trying to work for. One step closer to achieving success, right? Of course, you want to move forward and achieve your goal immediately!

Rarely does that work, if ever. Let us pause for a moment. Put yourself in the shoes of the individual you would like to meet. Imagine someone trying to meet you solely for information. Would you want someone to approach you with only one goal in mind, with only one reason to meet? The answer is a resounding no.

For this reason, it is important not to talk about what you need, what you want. Approach networking with the objective of building trust, growing confidence and friendship. Like setting the frame for a perfect photograph, you'll find that if you are patient, you'll find the perfect opportunity to present your case. Networking has better long-term benefits if you wait for the appropriate opportunity instead of rushing towards your own goals.

A sturdy network is built the same way a good friendship is: mutual trust, building on common interest, and investing good will. All of these are subjective goals. But they are the ingredients in establishing a strong bond with others who matter. Business and career benefits are secondary results of strong relationships built on trust.

Building trust is hard and establishing a strong relationship takes time. Ask yourself whether you will marry a person and decide to spend the rest of your life with them after meeting them only once. The few cases where this happens, like in romance novels, are the exceptions that prove the rule. To establish a strong connection where another party understands you well cannot happen in one seating. You need to work a relationship with a higher up the same way you work a relationship with a future life mate.

Sometimes I will invite persons who want to meet me for an eighteen-hole golf game. At the very first tee, before we even had a chance to finish the first hole, they get down to business and make their pitch. What are we supposed to do for the remaining seventeen holes? What if I do not like the business idea? Am I supposed to now fake a relationship and bear their presence for the rest of the game? This cold way to approach a relationship is damaging.

Take time to know the person you are networking with. Understand each other's ideas and objectives, build trust, and then brainstorm future collaborations. All of these happen over the course of many interactions. Go into a networking event with the mindset that the event is one step in many to come. You will then not try to achieve everything in that one meeting, rush your objectives and burn bridges. These hasty actions lead to a weak networking strategy.

Step #8: Refresh your network

I keep all my business cards in a big shoebox. Every other year, I go through that shoebox and I toss a large number of the cards away. In fact, I toss away more cards than I keep. People change roles all the time and our relationships with them change too. Further, we gather more information on people as time goes by. To keep a network healthy, pruning the network is as important as adding to the network. It is important that you take a look at your network at least once every year and decide who you should 'un-friend'. This is not a mean thing to do—it is a wise thing to do. One of the issues I have with large social network sites like Facebook and LinkedIn is that they do not encourage un-friending as much as they encourage friending. An unruly large network is very inefficient. A great network is like a bonsai tree—it is healthiest and lasts longest when it is carefully pruned. A network is worthy if it is selective.

Let's Play Golf

When I was ushered into Mr. O'Rourke's office that day, I found him to be an affable gentleman. He had read my friend's email and my application and wanted to see me in person to make sure I was indeed who I said I was.

He greeted me with a broad smile and a warm handshake. Even though our backgrounds were very different, we connected right away. After a few pleasantries and some questions, Mr. O'Rourke quickly realized that I had enough experiences and could bring enough opportunities to contribute to the club's reputation. Within ten minutes of meeting him, he casually said, "Well, if you want to become a member of the club, you need to understand the course. Let's play golf this weekend!" That would be my initiation into the club!

Once I joined, Tracy introduced me to several other key club members and I was able to quickly make inroads in the local business network. It was a life-changing opportunity for me.

CHAPTER 9: THE ORCHESTRA OF LEADERSHIP

"Being a conductor is kind of a hybrid profession because most fundamentally, it is being someone who is a coach, a trainer, an editor, a director."
Michael Tilson Thomas, Music Director of the San Francisco Symphony

"Being a director or a conductor is a balance of many things. And to do it right is a very difficult tightrope to walk. I've come to the conclusion that there's really no way to be one hundred percent popular as conductor."
Joshua Bell, Violinist and Music Director of the Academy of St Martin in the Fields

"Moral reasons are the tail wagged by the intuitive dog."
Jonathan Haidt, author The Happiness Hypothesis

An Almost Spiritual Experience

I must have been nine years old when it happened, but I still distinctly remember the day as if it happened yesterday. My friend had invited me over to his home to listen to music; he had a gramophone. In those days, not many people in Daegu had a gramophone— it was a luxury that only the rich or the music aficionados could afford. So after school, I paid him a visit and was captivated when I saw the music device in my friend's living room.

My friend's parents loved classical music and had built a small collection of vinyl records that were the prize possessions of the family and were kept in a small glass case next to the gramophone. Because of my great excitement and fascination with this beautiful device, my friend agreed to show me how the machine worked.

He picked one of the records, placed it on the turntable, and turned the power switch on. The disc started spinning in an almost trance-like fashion. He then lowered the tone arm and as soon as the pickup cartridge touched the disc, the music that played through the horn and filled the room reverberated through my heart. I learned much later that it had been Beethoven's Fifth Symphony—I had not known of Beethoven or any of the classic composers at the time—but the music immediately spoke to me.

I had never experienced anything like this before. To say that I was mesmerized by the music is an understatement. I was, in fact, hypnotized. As I listened, it felt as if the room and my friend next to me receded in the background. Everything around me faded away. The symphony pulled me in and transported me into a different realm.

I was experiencing a new reality. All my senses were peaked. The music was pouring into my whole body. I could almost pick up each and every instrument in the orchestra. I felt the whole and also felt the parts. I savored the music but could appreciate the individual instruments. And I could sense the music reverberating deep inside me. My nerves were firing rapidly and the symphony permeated my very being. By the end of the first movement, I had what I could call a spiritual experience.

When I returned home that evening, I walked straight to my room and lay down on the bed. I could not comprehend what had happened to me. How could a melody composed in the early 1800s in Vienna by a man who was in his mid-thirties and who was going deaf so deeply affect me, a young boy in Korea, more than one and a half a century later? Was it the novelty of the gramophone? Was it the deep beauty of the symphony? Was it the timeless composition of the allegro movements? Or, was it the transcendence of the art? I felt incapacitated.

Over the next several days, that feeling did not abate. In fact, I became more mystified, more puzzled, more bewildered. My parents, not knowing what was going through my mind, thought I was sick. They prescribed, like many parents still do today, more rest and warm soup. When they learned that it was my listening to classical music that led to this state of mind, they banned me from listening to music altogether.

The restriction was futile. I made more and more trips to my friend's house to listen to that magical device. Over the years since, I constantly seek out opportunities to revel in classical music and relive the experience. I would also discover that I had perceptive senses and an ability to sense the minutest details of an experience.

A Theory of the Mind

Jonathan Haidt, social psychologist and Professor at New York University, introduced the analogy of "the Elephant and the Rider" in his book *The Happiness Hypothesis*. Professor Haidt argues that the human mind comprises of an emotional, automatic, irrational side (the Elephant) and an analytical, controlled, rational side (the Rider).

In this metaphor, the puny Rider is unmatched in almost all aspects when compared to the large Elephant. Haidt adopts the Elephant analogy from Buddha, who symbolized the uncontrolled mind by a gray elephant that can run wild at any moment and destroy everything in its way.

The Rider has limited control on what the Elephant can do. Hence, in this model we humans are largely driven by our intuitions. Our rational mind only comes up with reasons, often post-hoc, after decisions have been made, to justify our intuitions. Haidt's theory is not necessarily a new one.

Termed social intuitionism, it is however an important departure from previous models that portrayed humans as rational and logical beings. The human mind, it turns out, relies extensively on intuitions and this is an evolutionary trait deeply ingrained in our genes.

Private reflection, which I call Wonder in my first book, is the only means by which rational thoughts can influence our intuitions. In general, intuition influences reason. As David Hume famously said, "Reason is, and ought only to be the slave of the passions, and can never pretend to any other office than to serve and obey them."

Understanding this theory of the mind is important to understanding how we derive reasons and make decisions. Our senses pick up clues from our environment. Our mind first derives intuitions based on those clues.

Our genetic predispositions, past experiences, cultural contexts, and social milieus influence these intuitions. Then, our mind comes up with reasons to justify these intuitions. So, the order is sensory followed by intuition followed by reason. The point I am trying to make then is this: an ability to fine tune our senses fine tunes our intuitive understanding of our circumstances, and better intuitions in turn improve our rational decisions.

I was born with highly alert senses, as I realized from experiencing classical music in my early years. However, I never once took this to be a bane. Rather, over the years, I further developed other senses to pick up minute details in my environment. I consciously developed a keen sense of seeing and sensing details. I took up photography for that very reason.

Whenever I travel I bring my Leica camera with me and I seek details on the streets of the cities I visit. I chose the Leica brand because it is the ideal camera for capturing life in the open. Shades, hues, tints, tones and, of course, bright colors catch my eye easily. I have trained myself to pick up on these variances. I like to take pictures of everyday life, such as people at a park, shadows in an alley, or a busy market. My friends have given me the title "paparazzi of strangers"! I capture these moments and then look for uniqueness in them—truly trying to see the world from different angles.

I rely a lot on my senses and my intuitions to arrive at decisions in both my personal and business life. A practice that I adopted since my early days in Silicon Valley and that I use even today is to go fifteen minutes early to an appointment with a party I am meeting for the first time.

I would often insist on meeting start-ups who are seeking investment or looking for consulting advice in their office. I would then show up unannounced fifteen minutes early and sit in their waiting room outside of the conference room.

In these fifteen minutes, I put my senses to work. I can smell the air in the environment, listen to the secretary talk on the phone, and pick up on the energy or lack thereof of employees walking by. I observe casual interactions of employees with the secretary, detect frustration or excitement in people's voices, and in general feel any harmony and dissonance in the office.

These sensory inputs come to my brain and intermingle with my repository of experiences and allow me to form a quick first intuition of the company. I have found out that these first intuitions are rarely wrong for me. As I said, I have trained my senses over the years to pick up on details and I have come to rely and trust on my mind signals.

By the time I am called into the meeting I have already formed a first opinion of the company. The burden is then on the leaders of the company to make a rational case to change my intuition. That, as we have found above, is no easy task.

It Starts with the CEO

One day I received a call from one of my mentees. Jason was looking to switch from his high-paying position in a multinational company for a new job in the startup space. He had found a position in a startup and called to ask for my advice and referral. The industry was in a crowded marketplace, but Jason and I researched the company. We found that the CEO and founder had a solid track record. The caliber of the CEO is always a key success indicator for me, so I made the referral and encouraged Jason to pursue the position.

The CEO reached out to me in response to the referral I made for Jason. At that time, I was traveling in Asia and he had to call me several times to get in touch. He was in Silicon Valley, but he always made sure to call between two to three a.m. in Californian time so that we could talk at a time that was comfortable for me. I was impressed—this is a sign of a good leader, being conscientious. And I could immediately tell by the way the CEO talked that he was a doer and an incredibly smart guy. So when Jason started off in the job, I knew he was aligned with an excellent leader.

Now, a starting a company is not for the faint of heart. The work load is nearly twenty hours a day. The competition is intense. It is as if one is piloting an Air Force jet and every moment is focused on maneuvering inside a tiny cockpit where the smallest action can have the biggest consequences. Sixth months in, the company was moving fast. Jason contacted me. He wanted to talk. He had a large checklist of questions, but he really wanted to complain. It would be easier to be the husband of a king's daughter! This job was too difficult, he could not handle the pressure. I was surprised, but I told him no—you cannot leave. Stay there. I asked him to be patient. I knew the quality of his work was good and I trusted my gut instinct about his strengths. I also knew that the CEO would deliver. He would be successful.

Twelve months passed, and Jason called again. He was exhausted. And again, he talked about quitting. He pleaded with me, he really wanted to quit. He had not slept, he was working day and night. He was not capable of doing the job. He wanted to move on. Again, I said no. I told him he must stay, he must believe in himself, work through this, and make his contribution. He would be rewarded. I had faith that he would succeed. There were things I could see from an outsider's perspective that Jason could not. I saw that the CEO was leading them to success, that the company would do well.

Two years later, Jason called and thanked me profusely. After two years of hard work, pushing through the difficult times, the company was bought out by one of the world's largest corporations in the industry and news was everywhere about the acquisition. Jason stayed the course, he was persistent, and he was rewarded beyond the expected return. The CEO had led the company to a financially successful outcome, just as I knew he would.

The Leader is a Maestro

If our reasons and decisions are influenced by intuitions and if those intuitions are formed by the cues we pick up through our senses, then it follows that a good leader making good decisions need to be able to pick up on the details in their surroundings.

This ability to sense nuances in an environment or in a discussion does not always come naturally. However, it is an ability that can be cultivated and learned as you experience different transformations of Geography, Emotion, Experience, Profession, and Reason. For that reason, I like to think of a leader as a maestro. Let us go back to the symphony example.

The Berlin Philharmonic is consistently ranked as one of the best orchestras in the world. Consisting of over a hundred musicians in concert, the orchestra is a true master when it comes to playing Beethoven. Founded in 1882, it has a long history and is closely associated with the history of the city itself. Its main venue, the Philharmonic, located in the Kulturforum area of Berlin, is an architectural masterpiece. The group, however, travels worldwide to play to houses with full audiences.

The conductor, or maestro, of the Berlin Philharmonic is Sir Simon Rattle. Sir Rattle has led the orchestra since 2002 and is regularly regarded as one of the best, if not the best, conductors in the world. Sir Rattle's approach to the orchestra as a coordinated group producing a wonderfully pleasing product has many lessons for the aspiring leader.

First, consider the difficulty of his task. He leads in concert a very large number of musicians playing a variety of instruments: violin, viola, cello, double bass, flute, oboe, clarinet, bassoon, horn, trumpet, trombone, tuba, timpani, percussion and harp.

Standing in front of this group, he needs to guide them, cue them, and lead them in an expertly synchronized manner. He has to be extremely aware of the performance of each member of the orchestra. And he needs to decide on the spot what to correct and who to correct to keep the beautiful symphony flowing.

Sir Rattle's ability to discern the slightest nuance in the various streams of music reaching his ears and other senses is critical. In this role, he does not need to know how to play each piece of equipment. However, he needs to be able to sense the whole orchestra and lead them accordingly.

A leader such as a CEO has a similar task. They do not need to know how to perform the task of each and every employee in the company. But, they need to be acutely aware of the various streams of information that can reach them. They need to be able to decipher the variety and understand the details in their immediate surrounding. They need to be able to pick up on faint signs and signals. And they need to be able to respond in real-time. They need, as explained above, to develop acute senses of their surroundings.

Similarly, the orchestra is like a company. Every musician has a critical role to play but they only achieve greatness if they can work together with the rest of the group. Only when the individual musician plays their part at the right time, with a lot of practice, at the right pitch, right volume, and right timbre, in tune with the rest of their teammates can they produce the most beautiful of sounds. And a team that produces an innovative product, like Beethoven's music, has the potential to appeal to a large percentage of humanity across cultures and across time.

Sir Rattle is an exemplary leader outside of the concert hall as well. Before joining the Berlin Philharmonic, he pushed for more artistic independence of the orchestra from the Berlin Senate and he lobbied for an increase in the salary of the musicians. In fact, he refused to sign his contract unless these demands were met. In doing so, he sent a strong message showing that he values freedom of action and decision and that he wants to have a satisfied and happy team working for him. Sir Rattle's tenure, during which he has recorded both classical and contemporary music, has been very well received.

Good leaders rely on their senses. They cultivate an ability to detect small signals in their environment, whether these are sights, smells, or sounds. I enjoy going to malls and large stores simply to walk around and visually take in all the display around me. These sensory inputs inform our intuitions and, as research shows and as David Hume observed, intuitions guide our reasons and decisions.

A maestro leading an orchestra is a good example of a leader who has fine-tuned their senses to detect how a large group doing a multitude of simultaneous yet different tasks can be led to perform well and produce an excellent product. Aspiring leaders should develop this ability to pick up nuanced cues around them. These cues, multiplied by experience, enable leaders to make quick gut feeling decisions. And once the cues start, leaders should stay focused on that course of action—there is no good plan B. By honing this ability to appreciate and detect minute details, leaders improve on the accuracy of their decisions.

CHAPTER 10: EVERYONE IS PART OF THE GAME

"Capitalism is the only system that can make freedom, individuality, and the pursuit of values possible in practice. When I say 'capitalism,' I mean a pure, uncontrolled, unregulated laissez-faire capitalism—with a separation of economics, in the same way and for the same reasons as a separation of state and church."
Ayn Rand

"Those of us who have looked to the self-interest of lending institutions to protect shareholders' equity, myself included, are in a state of shocked disbelief."
Alan Greenspan to the House Committee on Oversight and Government Reform in 2008

"If you put the federal government in charge of the Sahara Desert, in 5 years there'd be a shortage of sand."
Nobel Laureate Milton Friedman

"Our insatiable appetite for fossil fuels and the corporate mandate to maximize shareholder value encourages drilling without taking into account the costs to the ocean, even without major spills."
Sylvia Earle, National Geographic's Explorer-in-Residence

A Recipe with Many Ingredients

People often call me a successful investor but they don't know my real score card. I think I have missed the target more than I hit the bullseye by eight to two, but luckily some of the hits had a pretty hefty return so I have no complaints. Money making has not been my ultimate goal anyway. My goal has always been a happy life by helping and sharing with the younger generation.

When I look at other successful entrepreneurs, there are quite a few of them who became very rich by just one stroke. Some went straight to retirement in their twenties. On the surface, it seems unfair if I compare that with my twenty years of investment in multiple companies and projects. However, I have never thought that way because I know what I am good at and what I'm not – I know If I started a company and settled in for too long in the CEO's office, it might just be out of business in six months! I can be a nagger with a micro-management style and I don't know how many people would still be around me after a few months!

I definitely give founders who stay with their company long-term huge credit. Creating or fixing a business is one thing. Growing it over the years to become a global empire requires many special skills and unique talent which I don't have. So I would like to admit that I have been just fortunate to have met many amazing entrepreneurs and to have participated in their successes in my lifetime.

There are really many different skillsets needed to create a successful company. Visionaries and doers. Subject matter experts and experts managing teams. The list is long and we need to know where we fit and who else we need to round out our teams.

In order to adapt quickly to changes in the business world, a workforce needs to be flexible. And to quickly shift a business in different directions, leaders must intimately understand all the key transactions in their business as well as have a deep understanding of the individuals who performs these transactions.

In many corporations, I see that the CEO has not worked their way from the ground up. They have attended the right schools, belong to the right clubs. But they do not know what it means to be a sales associate. Many times, decisions are made that do not reflect or support the very core of how a business model makes money— from the company associate to the customer.

It should be required for executives to intimately know all the major parts that influence the core transactions. Important information can be found at all echelons of an organization. First, start off by treating everyone with respect. Only then will you get honest answers. Second, put yourself in the shoes of your workers. If you want to understand your workforce and how best to control those forces, then you must understand the worker and challenges they face.

When you put yourself in others' shoes, that is another way to expand awareness. Take for example the popular TV show *Undercover Boss*. This show has the CEO of a popular company go undercover as a sales or customer associate. The CEO learns how to make a burger or taco, run point on an assembly line, or even clean bathrooms. The CEO learns the daily activities that influence and impact the key employee responsible for everyday customer transactions.

In every single show, the CEO learns valuable information. They learn how to improve the transaction from both the representative's viewpoint and also how to increase customer satisfaction. This understanding helps to drive up overall sales by addressing issues involved in the transaction.

As an example of this, T-Mobile USA had a program where executive management was required to spend a few days in the shoes of a customer service or sales rep. During these days, directors and higher up executives would ring up sales in a local store or they would take calls from the customer and try to resolve an issue.

However, it can be difficult to take the time to truly understand all aspects of your business when a quarterly earnings report is looming. Sometimes short-term profits make a more compelling case for shortcuts as there is incredible pressure to produce growth and profits. Leadership is all about defining success for your company and setting the path to get there. And on this path, leaders have competing priorities to balance and many voices clamoring for attention. Perhaps one of the biggest dilemmas a CEO will face is figuring out what is truly in the best interest of the company.

What They Need Is...

In 1962, Milton Friedman, economist and soon-to-be Nobel Prize laureate, published his seminal book – *Capitalism and Freedom*. He discussed what is now known as the Friedman Doctrine, the idea that the singular goal of a company is to increase its shareholders' value. A company should only need to be responsible for its shareholders and not anyone else.

He wrote, "there is one and only one social responsibility of business — to use its resources and engage in activities designed to increase its profits so long as it stays within the rules of the game, which is to say, engages in open and free competition without deception or fraud."

It rests on solid economics and mathematics: selling more, increasing revenue, and decreasing costs are the three profit levers of a company.

In the four decades since Friedman published his book, "maximizing shareholder value" has become a mantra in the corporate world. Everybody from executives in the corporate world to editors of business newspapers to MBA Professors at the top business schools sang its tune.

There was plenty of evidence that a sharp focus on eliminating soft expenses could improve a company's economic performance. Take IBM as an example. In the early 1990s IBM faced an existential crisis. The legendary company that had propelled America and the world into a technological era was on the verge of collapse.

Lou Gerstner, who had made a name for himself at American Express, McKinsey, and RJR Nabisco was brought in to save the company. Soon he published IBM's new set of principles and a focus on shareholder value was high on that list. He went on to eliminate 60,000 jobs—one of the biggest layoffs in American history. The company's stocks bounced back and Gerstner was hailed as a turnaround genius and was handsomely compensated.

Fanatics of the Friedman Doctrine saw any expense by an organization that did not result in a direct increase in profits as a cost. Should a company spend on programs that boost employee morale? Sponsor a local park? Give to charity? Extreme believers in the Shareholder theory feel that the answer to these questions should be a loud "No."

In the early 2000s though the U.S. was reeling from a series of large scandals at Enron, Global Crossing, ImClone, Tyco International, and WorldCom, and pundits, professors and politicians were all arguing that a singular focus on maximizing profits was causing managers to introduce practices in their operations that were often self-serving and risky.

Alan Greenspan, then Chairman of the Federal Reserve, testifying in front of Congress said, "this modern risk-management paradigm held sway for decades. The whole intellectual edifice, however, collapsed in the summer of last year." The pressure to generate profits had caused an overemphasis on short-term stock performance over long-term gains. The Shareholder theory was like a nitrous oxide shot into a car's engine: it could give a corporation a short-term high acceleration along a short straight track but was dangerous when the car needs to negotiate a long bendy road.

Of course profit is important. But is there different approach that might be more effective? More recently business executives have been dusting off another book on their shelves. In 1984 Professor Edward Freeman at the Darden School of the University of Virginia proposed the Stakeholder theory in his book *Strategic Management: A Stakeholder's Approach*. In it he identifies the various groups that a company should keep in mind as it goes about its business. The groups are divided into two: internal stakeholders and external stakeholders. The internal stakeholders include the company's employees, managers, and owners. The external stakeholders include the society, government, creditors, shareholders, suppliers, and customers. In other words, there is an entire ecosystem that makes a business successful.

The firm is a big network with many nodes – when all the nodes are strong and stable, the network is strong and stable too. It is like a football game, or really any team sport at all. Every player in the team has a unique responsibility to deliver their best. When one person makes a slight error, the team often ends up losing the game. The corporation of tomorrow operates its many functions like the body operates its many limbs and parts—if one of them is hurting, the whole body is in pain. The body as a whole must be looked after and kept healthy.

We now know that a negative social media review on one department or a negative blog post by a disgruntled employee impacts customers' perception of the whole company. Subpar working conditions in a factory in Asia impact profitability of the company in the malls in America.

There is evidence that the Stakeholder theory works. Take Walmart as an example. For decades, the company's strategy was to cut costs wherever they could find them. It squeezed pennies out of every operation. It's motto for a long time was "Always Low Prices." With over 5,000 stores in the United States alone and 2.3 million employees worldwide, wages were a major factor in Walmart's book of expenses.

Walmart infamously kept wages so low that labor groups accused it of depressing wages across the entire American economy. And that cost-centric strategy worked for Walmart for a quite some time. However, in the past few years its fortunes took a sharp turn.

Beset by competition from both online and other brick-and-mortar retailers, its revenue fell in 2015 for the first time in forty-five years. The

New York Times wrote, "Shoppers (at Walmart) were fed up. They complained of dirty bathrooms, empty shelves, endless checkout lines and impossible-to-find employees. Only sixteen percent of stores were meeting the company's customer service goals."

The executives at Walmart's headquarters in Bentonville, Arkansas reflected on the issues facing the company and decided to adopt a series of solutions that surprised everybody. They understood that the cost-cutting measures had gone too far. In a break from tradition, they proposed to reverse the slide by adopting measures that would make their employees happier and feel more valued.

COO Judith McKenna said, "We realized quickly that wages are only one part of it (the problem), that what also matters are the schedules we give people, the hours that they work, the training we give them, the opportunities you provide them. What you've got to do is not just fix one part, but get all of these things moving together."

Walmart raised employee wages across the board. Minimum wage was no longer the threshold that guided their hiring process. The company set up 200 training centers to train employees and offered them a promotion path to management roles. Walmart's CEO Doug McMillon said in a statement to the employees, "It's clear to me that one of the highest priorities today must be an investment in you, our associates."

By late summer 2016, the initiatives taken by Walmart were paying off. Customer surveys improved, showing a steady incline in customer satisfaction. Revenue was up at the most vulnerable stores too, those that were recently opened. Regarding the employees, Ms. McKenna said, "Our associates are an asset. You don't try to have the very lowest cost of an asset. You try to have the right asset. So rather than thinking about the lowest cost, the question is how you get the best productivity."

Some companies have been taking even more drastic measures to reward their employees. Chobani is a company founded in 2005 by Turkish immigrant Hamdi Ulukaya. The company sells a line of yogurt that has been warmly welcomed by the American consumer. The valuation of the company stands at a likely $7 billion today.

In April 2016, Mr. Ulukaya took a step that gained him praises from labor groups and customers alike: he handed over ten percent of the company's shares to his employees. Mr. Ulukaya said, "I've built something I never thought would be such a success, but I cannot think of Chobani being built without all these people. Now they'll be working to build the company even more and building their future at the same time."

Another company, Gravity Payments, gained notoriety in April of 2015 by declaring the minimum wage of the company would be $70,000. In order to accomplish this, the CEO reduced his own million-dollar salary to $70,000. As a result, six thousand new accounts were secured. Employees were happy and committed to the company.

But then there was backlash. One prominent finance employee quit, saying the raise was unfair to upper level employees who have sacrificed long hours for the company. The CEO was also sued by his brother (who owned thirty percent of the company) who claimed that he purposefully diminished the financial state in order to avoid paying out his portion.

How is this company two years later? Gravity Payments is enjoying rapid growth. They doubled their work space. Employees are contributing to the economy in a significant way by being able to purchase homes and vehicles. Workers even pooled their money to buy a new Tesla for their CEO. Dan Price's decision to give employees a massive pay increase created a workplace where the employees treat each minute decision as if they were the owner. That kind of loyalty has a benefit that The Friedman Doctrine did not take into account.

Many other companies have also adopted what are termed "Corporate Social Responsibility (CSR)" initiatives. These are initiatives that hold the companies responsible for their actions and encourage positive contributions to the environment and the communities they operate in.

Examples of CSR include companies insisting on the use of renewable energies in their buildings, setting up employee donation matching programs, and directly contributing to their local community. As an example, since 1946, Target has supported the communities in which they have stores. Over the past several years, the company's efforts, from growing sustainable practices to providing educational grants, have amounted to five percent of its profit going to local communities. Target proudly advertises that it donates $4 million each week to its communities. Since 2010, the company has donated more than $875 million towards education alone.

So, should CEOs focus on shareholders or stakeholders? Costs or benefits? We teach our executives to let data drive logical decisions, measure and optimize every aspect of the company. But this worldview alone can place reason above emotions, objectivity above subjectivity, and hard metrics of achievements over soft indicators of success. The world is a complex arena with many moving parts that are often outside of our control. Human emotions cannot quite be cleanly explained or defined.

Values can be more persuasive than functionality, and soft goals might be more nebulous, yet give us a more comprehensive definition of success.

In my personal opinion, a worldview that pushes for strict data-driven theories to improve efficiencies, like the Friedman Doctrine, is good in the short-term only. These theories also require an overall system that is mature in many other areas. You cannot implement a Libertarian economic policy in a country that has no fair judiciary, no independent press, and corrupt politics as an example.

For a long-term view, it is necessary to consider a broader theory, like the Stakeholder theory, which encompasses a more comprehensive approach. By keeping all stakeholders' benefits in mind, a company is able to "increase the size of the pie." Even if it appears that a smaller percentage of profits are being directed to the shareholders, in reality the overall profits may be higher and hence the profits to the shareholders and other stakeholders, higher as well.

As you plan your strategies in your businesses, big or small, I encourage you to think broadly and consider comprehensive approaches to solving your challenges. Think long-term without losing sight of the short term.

The performance of a business is elevated by the quality of its talent, and in recent years we see forward-thinking organisations use all ways and means to recruit and retain top millenials. An exciting and open culture not only attracts top talent, but also challenges and inspires its people to perform better. Look at all your stakeholders, internal and external, and design solutions that improve the lot of everybody. A rising tide lifts all boats goes the old adage.

CHAPTER 11: TOP 10 IRREPLACEABLE CEOS

"In order to be irreplaceable one must always be different."
Fashion designer Coco Chanel

"The CEO is chief worrier and chief cheerleader."
Stein Kruse, CEO of Holland America Group

"Success breeds complacency. Complacency breeds failure.
Only the paranoid survive."
Andy Grove, Founder and CEO of Intel

The Traits of an Irreplaceable Leader

In my first book, *Wonder*, I posed the question, what makes companies last forever? In other words, what enables a company to repeatedly and continually be successful? What allows a company to remain relevant to generations of customers? One can ask a parallel question: what makes a CEO repeatedly and continually successful? What makes a CEO desirable by all the stakeholders of a company for as long as they desire to work? What makes a CEO irreplaceable?

There are many factors that make CEOs successful—a great team, a proven company culture, a network of partners, a hit product, a favorable market environment, a fan base of loyal customers, perfect timing, luck, etc. The list goes on and on. However, these are all to a large extent external to the CEO. They are factors that if channeled correctly can be made available to all CEOs. In my view, there are internal factors that are more important than these external factors to the repeated and continual success of the CEO. Internal factors are personal traits of the CEO—habits, behaviors, characters that set them apart. Personal traits determine how well the CEO can leverage the external factors to ensure their long-term success—to become truly irreplaceable.

Many people still rank Steve Jobs as probably the most irreplaceable CEO of our time. And the fact that Apple seems to be faltering after he is gone further proves this point.

Many of you could pick your own favorites but this is my personal list. Let me share my top ten.

1. SIR JAMES DYSON, DYSON LTD

Many words describe Sir James Dyson, founder of the Dyson company: innovative, designer extraordinaire, and visionary. But, I like to see Sir James through the personal trait of determination— grit, courage and resolution to get things done. Growing up in England, Sir James was a long-distance runner. He once said, "I was quite good at it (long distance running), not because I was physically good, but because I had more determination. I learnt determination from it." This determination to wait longer, go farther, fight harder will reward Sir Dyson tremendously in his career. Today, his net worth is $5 billion and it is said that he owns more land in England than the Queen herself.

Sir James' most famous invention is undoubtedly the bagless vacuum cleaner that uses the technology of cyclonic separation to pick up dirt without losing suction with the floor. Sir James came up with this idea in the 1970s. He spent a full five years prototyping the design before launching the "G-Force" cleaner in 1983. However, the existing manufacturers and distributors at the time refused to carry the G-Force as they saw it a threat to the dust bag replacement model.

The vacuum cleaner companies were convincing the end users that the replacement dust bags are an efficient way to operate the cleaners—use and throw instead of manually cleaning the cleaners. So, Sir James Dyson launched the product in Japan through catalogue sales. There sales picked up and he received the International Design Fair prize in 1991. In 1993, he opened a research center in the UK. It was not until 1997 that the vacuum cleaners would become the fastest selling cleaners in the UK. Dyson was also the first company to offer five-year guarantees for their cleaners, because Sir James believed that "If anyone has a problem with our product, we have a problem." And in 2005, Dyson would lead vacuum cleaner sales as measured by revenue in the United States. That is a thirty-five-year history! Throughout this journey, Sir James never gave up. He kept on believing, kept on running, kept on inventing and in the end, he has been richly rewarded. His disruptive innovations continue and he has plans to introduce electric cars to compete with Tesla and many others. I'm sure we will see many more ideas from Sir James.

2. MARC BENIOFF, SALESFORCE.COM

Great thinkers can envision a world that challenges all existing norms. They have an uncanny ability to question the present as it is. And they have the courage to propose an alternate better model. Consider this: in 1905, Albert Einstein published not one, not two but four extraordinary papers that would overturn our understanding of matter, energy and mass. Einstein had the intellectual fortitude and the moral courage to challenge centuries of Newtonian Physics. And we are all better off because of him. In science as in business, every now and then a thinker arises who challenges the natural order of things. Marc Benioff, founder of Salesforce.com, is one such leader.

Marc Benioff was born in San Francisco. Silicon Valley was in his DNA. At a young age, he became interested in technology and all things computers. While in high school, he developed and sold his first software – an instruction set on how to juggle that ran on the TRS-80 microcomputer from Tandy Corporation (forerunner of RadioShack). He made $75. At the age of 15, he founded a software company and wrote games for the Atari 800. By age 16, he was making enough money from the licensing revenue from these games to pay his way to college. While at the University of Southern California, Marc took an internship at Apple working as a software programmer in the Macintosh Division under cofounder Steve Jobs. Jobs would remain an inspiration to Marc for the rest of his life. After graduating from USC, he took a job at Oracle and climbed the ladder quickly. In addition to his sharp technical mind, Marc also had a keen sense of marketing and business. He learnt the ropes of serving the customer from his father who owned a department store in San Francisco. By the time he was 26, Marc was a Vice President at Oracle and was making $300,000 a year! He grew close to the founder of Oracle, Larry Ellison, and the two not only worked but also travelled the world together. Clearly, software made Marc as Marc was making software.

Yet, Marc was an oracle onto himself. Born, raised and fed on software, Marc had a vision beyond software. He took a sabbatical from his corporate gig and started to dream of a company whose motto would be "No Software!" Marc, in this way, is a visionary like Einstein. While the rest of the world deeply believed in the software model, Marc foresaw a world with no software. His company, Salesforce.com, would reinvent the way software is delivered to enterprise customers. Traditionally, companies like Oracle, installed large servers on premises at their customers' sites. Marc saw many disadvantages in this model – every customer required almost a unique solution at their site since each had its own unique needs and problems. Instead, Marc thought of a solution where no software is delivered on premises but rather the customers access the software remotely through a browser. He had envisioned the now commonplace

Software-As-A-Service (SAAS) model. At first nobody took him very seriously. He went to dozens of venture capitalists on Sandy Hill road and they all kicked him out. How could investors who have become rich on software see a world of no software? How could scientists who have become famous on Newtonian Physics see a world beyond Newton? Convince of his idea, Marc raised money privately from friends he knew. Larry Ellison gave him money. So did Nancy Pelosi's family. Equipped with a most unconventional vision, Marc would take Salesforce.com on a revolutionary trajectory. The company went public in 2004 and today is worth close to $70B and growing.

Today Marc spends considerable time on charitable and philanthropic causes. He has lobbied for equal rights for minority groups and has invested in dozens of startups. He is a great leader because he has the ability to envision an alternate world, the boldness to question the status quo and the courage to go on when everybody else rejects him. Marc is irreplaceable.

3. Chung Ju-Yung, Hyundai

If I had to pick one person in the business world that I respected most, by far I would pick Mr. Chung Ju-Yung, the founder of Hyundai Group. Mr. Chung Ju-Yung was born in Korea under Japanese rule. He passed away at the age of eighty-five in 2008. He is the only CEO in this chapter who made his mark primarily in the past century. However, I know of no other CEO who has demonstrated the character of re-invention better that Mr. Chung Ju-Yung. Let us all learn from this great man.

Mr. Chung was born in dire poverty in North Korea at a time when vast areas of the country were poor and struggling. His initial dream was to become a schoolteacher but he could not get the education to achieve even this humble goal. So, at a very young age, Mr. Chung left his family home and went to other towns to find work. He literally was running from home to change the story of his life.

At age sixteen, he walked fifteen miles to Kowon and worked as a construction worker. At age eighteen, he ran away again from home and made his way to Seoul where he found a job in a rice shop. His work ethics impressed the owner so much that after a few years the owner left him the shop.

That new responsibility, life experience, and a tenacious attitude set Mr. Chung on a path of never-ending success. At age twenty-five, he took a loan and started a mechanic shop. That would mark his entry into a space that he would later pioneer as the founder and chairman of Hyundai Group, a conglomeration that included Hyundai Automotive Group, Hyundai Construction group, Hyundai Department Retail Group, Hyundai Heavy Industries Group and many more.

Mr. Chung has many remarkable achievements during his lifetime. Some of these are big accomplishments impacting the national identity of South Korea and some of these achievements are memorable stories with deep lessons for all of us to learn and ponder. Here is one story in particular that makes me always smile whenever I think of it.

Mr. Chung often would stay on the job-site for long periods of time. In one such stay, he had trouble sleeping because the place was infested with fleas. The fleas were a nuisance and were severely impacting the productivity of the site. Mr. Chung gave the problem some thought and after a few days finally came up with a solution—he set up a tall sleeping table in the middle of the room so no flea could jump onto it. For a while, the solution worked and Mr. Chung asked all of the construction workers to follow his solution. However, a few days later several workers came to him and told him that the fleas were biting again!

Mr. Chung investigated the issue with a flashlight in the middle of the night. His jaw dropped when he found out what was going on. The fleas were climbing up on the wall, crawling to the center of the ceiling and then dropping on the tables where the employees were sleeping! These tiny insects apparently outsmarted Mr. Chung! He could not believe that these little bugs came up with such a brilliant solution to their own problem!

After that, Mr. Chung would often joke to his employees that they were worse than fleas whenever they failed to come up with a solution to their problems! So, in the end, who won the war between Mr. Chung and the fleas? Mr. Chung was not one to give up. He came up with a new and better strategy. He set up a large bowl filled with water on the sleeping tables for a few days. And a miracle happened. Most of the fleas dived into the water throughout the night and drowned. It was like a fleas' death row! Mr. Chung's idea worked very successfully and soon all of fleas were eradicated from the job-site. In the end, Mr. Chung won the battle.

Over a long career, Mr. Chung worked many jobs and took on many roles. He kept re-inventing himself, always finding a means to push forward, to do something new, to take on fresh challenges. After his passing, the company has been struggling, which further demonstrates the central role he played in its success. One thing is for sure—if Mr. Chung were still alive, there is no doubt that the Hyundai Group and Korea would be a different landscape today. He is missed by all of Koreans as well and his lifetime stories will be told for many years to come.

4. JACK MA, ALIBABA AND JEFF BEZOS, AMAZON

I like to think about Jack Ma and Jeff Bezos as the Genghis Khan and Alexander of our times. They both have indomitable grit, boundless ambition and a desire to conquer the world, endlessly trying to capture a bigger share of the market. Mr. Ma is starting East and moving West and Mr. Bezos starting West and moving East. As they progress on their journey, they are redefining the landscape, changing our lives and, of course, amassing massive wealth. There is so much to say about them, and the speed and scale at which they effect change. It is challenging to keep up with them even in my writing – every time I finish writing, they would already have come up with something new! Like their conqueror forebears, both Mr. Ma and Mr. Bezos have their quirks, their grander-than-life image, their armies of loyal staff, their zealous cheerleaders and fans and their occasional oracles. Their inevitable and ultimate collision, when they both contend for the same market territory, will leave all of us in awe. As I am writing this in Dec 2017, some people are predicting that one of their empires will be the first to reach a trillion dollars in market capitalization, for the first time in human history. Perhaps by the time this book is released, it would already have happened. Their impact will be felt for generations to come.

Mr. Ma reminds me of a modern time Genghis Khan, who said "There is no good in anything until it is finished." Armies of journalists all over the world have poured into Mr. Ma's life, looking for what transformed this poor, thin, seemingly uncharacteristic teacher who used to earn a meager a salary of $12 per month to one of the richest men on the planet with a personal net worth in the billions of dollars! Here, I would like to focus on one trait that is talked about often and that is exemplified in Mr. Ma like in nobody else: persistence.

When he founded Alibaba, Mr. Ma pooled money from a group of friends. The company struggled for the first three years barely making any profit and almost falling into bankruptcy. Mr. Ma sought funding from forty different venture firms and they all rejected him. If there is one thing that is common in every step in Mr. Ma's career, it is not success but rather rejection. And persistence is the only tool to overcome rejections.

As of this writing, Alibaba generates billions of Chinese yuan per year. Their e-commerce portal has repeatedly processed sales in excess of one trillion yuan! Alibaba popularized November 11th, now known as 1111 and Singles' day, to be the Global Shopping Festival Day. On November 11 in 2017 Alibaba generated a record 168.2 billion yuan ($25.3 billion) in sales, as the e-commerce giant worked with traditional retailers to market everything from discounted lobster, iPhones and refrigerators to shoppers from at least 225 countries and regions. This idea was created by Mr. Ma by himself and truly he is a visionary.

As with Mr. Ma, gallons of ink have been poured by journalists and researchers alike to reverse engineer Mr. Jeff Bezos's success. What led to his meteoric rise? What enabled him to survive the dot-com bust when hundreds of other online retailers perished (remember webvan, anybody)? How is he able to repeatedly expand his business in areas nobody expected and make a killing there? Dozens of dissertations and countless books have been written to attempt to answer these questions. In my view, and as with Mr. Ma, the reason Mr. Bezos succeeded is due to the traits he shares with men like Alexander. He is meticulous, strategic, confident, persistent and extremely ambitious.

Mr. Bezos left a high-paying career on Wall Street, packed up his car, drove from New York to Seattle and wrote the business plan for Amazon along the way. He initially conceived of the company as an online bookstore, a convenient alternative to the down-the-street brick and mortar bookstore that has been around since papyrus was invented in ancient Egypt. The idea was neither novel nor complex. In fact, other entrepreneurs then (in the early 1990s) were attempting to sell books and everything else online. Internet technology was the new electricity. Its adoption was swift, its significance was mind-boggling and its promises staggering. It seemed like a new internet company was being formed every day. And, Amazon, it appears, was only one of a multitude. All that is true. What is also true, though, is that Mr. Bezos is one of his kind.

From the very beginning, Mr. Bezos saw in Amazon a company that would go far beyond selling books. Along the way, he expanded to selling retail items to every imaginable product on the planet. Today, more product searches are done on Amazon than on Google. This is very significant as a product search often leads to a paying event whereas an informational search most often does not. Then he repeatedly churned out new businesses from his own operations.

Once Amazon perfected storing data for their store online, Mr. Bezos made a business of cloud storage and marketed it as Amazon Web Services (AWS). Once the AWS platform became robust, he offered it for photo and personal data storage. Once the bandwidth problems were solved, he offered streaming videos. Once the videos picked up enough audience, he started contracting his own movies and is now a force in Hollywood. Once everybody was buying books online, he offered a digital format and the now indispensable kindle device. Once he entered the hardware space, he developed cellular phones and the now ubiquitous Alexa. And, that is not counting his foray into print media (Washington Post), brick-and-mortar stores (Wholefoods), self-check-out technologies (Amazon Go), drone deliveries (Amazon Air) and the list goes on. Even Walmart is struggling to compete.

So, very much like Alexander who would conquer a city and then draft its army to advance to the next city, Mr. Bezos has been steadily conquering market spaces, healthcare being his next foray. He will not stop until the world itself has been conquered. In fact, Mr. Bezos launched Blue Origin, a company building spacecraft, and have been rapidly expanding the company as of late. It appears that he has already set his sight beyond Earth! No company in the history of business has ever approached a value of 1 trillion dollars, but I predict that either Alibaba or Amazon will be the first. Perhaps by the time this book out, or in less than few years, one or both empires would have reached 1 trillion in market value!

5. INDRA NOOYI, PEPSI

Indra Nooyi has broken many glass ceilings in her life. Her mother never went to college and never worked outside of the home. Yet, her mother instilled a strong sense of confidence in her two daughters and laid the foundations for young Indra to become one of the most successful businesswomen of our time.

Ms. Nooyi earned management degrees from the prestigious Indian Institute of Management and from Yale. She worked for Boston Consulting Group, then at Motorola, and later for the Swedish-Swiss multinational Asea Brown Boveri before joining PepsiCo in 1994.

At PepsiCo, she climbed the corporate ladder working in a number of roles ranging from Strategic Planning to Corporate Strategy to CFO. In 2006, she was appointed President and CEO of the company and in 2007 she was made chairman of the board. Ms. Nooyi is the first female CEO of the storied company. She is also the first immigrant CEO of the company that was started in North Carolina more than a hundred years ago.

Ms. Nooyi has revisited PepsiCo's mission in a direction that many knew was needed but few dared to attempt: her "Performance with Purpose" strategy "promises to do what's right for the business by doing what's right for people and the planet." This is code word for pivoting a company known for making tasty but unhealthy snacks and sweetened drinks to one that provides more health-conscious options.

She has been quoted for being a 24/7 strategiser: "I wake up in the middle of the night and write different versions of PepsiCo on a sheet of paper." It is a gutsy move to redirect a whole culture towards a different kind of beverage when for over one hundred years a sugary drink defined the company. This pioneering step has proven to be the right bet for PepsiCo and a boon for the company in recent years.

For these initiatives and for her management style, Ms. Nooyi has received a very long list of accolades. Forbes magazine ranked her on their "World's 100 Most Powerful Women" for seven years in a row. Fortune magazine ranked her number one on their annual ranking of "Most Powerful Women in Business" for five years in a row. U.S. News & World Report named her as one of "America's Best Leaders." In her native country of India, she was named one of the "25 Greatest Global Living Legends" by NDTV, a popular media channel.

Ms. Nooyi truly embodies the pioneering spirit. She overcame countless possible biases against women, against mothers, and against immigrants to become the top leader of one of America's most recognizable brands globally. And once at the helm, she has continued to be a pioneer, charting and discovering new fertile grounds for an old company to rejuvenate itself.

6. MASAYOSHI SON, SOFTBANK

Masayoshi Son was born in a poor family in Japan in 1957. His father was a bootlegger, a pig farmer, and a restaurant owner. The family is of Korean ethnicity. That's what makes me proud as well. In those early post-war days, being the son of a poor minority farmer in Japan came with its struggles. However, Son had a spirit of adventure and always followed his instincts.

By the time he was sixteen, he came to the United States to study economics and computer science. While at university he was introduced to semiconductor technologies in Silicon Valley. His instincts immediately kicked in and he realized that microchips would power the technological revolution that was soon coming.

He started putting his mind to use and patented a method to use technology for translation. He then hired a few employees and got them to build a prototype device. He sold that device to Sharp and reinvested that money into his next startup. His instincts were already paying off.

Over his career, Son would make many instinctive calls. He would invest in companies based on his gut feelings. He invested in Yahoo!, Alibaba, Vodafone, Sprint, and recently acquired Saxby's ARM Holdings, the company we discussed above!

He invested in Sprint with an eye towards investing in T-Mobile and merging the two companies. He purchased ARM with an intention of powering the Internet of Things. In the former case, the United States government blocked a potential merger of two of America's largest service providers. In the latter case, the story is still unfolding. In all these cases, however, Son acts with what his former lieutenant Satoshi Shim says are his instincts.

Son started his first company at the age of nineteen. He set a very long-term vision then. In fact, he planned a fifty year strategy! The story goes that on the day he started his first company, Softbank, in 1981, he stood on 2 apple crates and gave an inspirational talk to his employees. He was excited and ambitious, and imagined his company to dominate the PC industry and be the number one company for software distribution. They listened, jaw-dropped, and then they both quit! But it appears that Son was far from unrealistic with his ambitions. Today, he owns 770 companies and 120 holdings generating over Y100B annually. And he is not slowing down any time soon. At Softbank company meeting, he announced that he sees the company growing even bigger. Son has the uncanny knack to be able to peek into tomorrow – he is a real visionary. He has the ability to know where companies and industries are going and he has an ability to make quick decisions on such bets. It is said that he invested in Alibaba after only 30 minutes of hearing their pitch. Son challenges himself and challenges his employees. He spends considerable time with junior leaders to groom them in his ways – risk taking with responsibility.

Along with a sense of careful diligence, a CEO needs to be able to trust his gut feelings, his inner compass, his instincts. In Son's case, many of his ventures failed. However, he is today the richest man in Japan and one of the richest men in the world. He now has a 300-year plan for the future, including investing in telepathic communication. I think we shouldn't bet against Son!

7. HOWARD SCHULTZ, STARBUCKS

The Canarsie Bayview Houses in Brooklyn, New York is a low-income housing project set up by the New York City Housing Authority. Like many housing projects in the New York boroughs, Bayview is too often a site of violent crime, with more than its

fair share of break-ins, shootings and murders. Often it is those who are struggling economically who choose to make the federally subsidized place their home out of economic necessity. This was where Howard Schultz grew up.

The Schultz patriarch worked several low-income jobs and none of them paid much money. Schultz' mother was a receptionist for a while and then spent her time raising the three children. One day, when Howard was very young, he walked into a room and found his father on the couch with a cast from his hip to his ankle. Shultz Senior was a delivery driver and he fell on a sheet of ice while picking up a load of dirty cloth diapers. Howard recounts the event as follows: "In those days you were dismissed from a job if you were injured. We didn't have health care and very little money to get by; my father never made more than $20,000 a year. What followed was an unbelievable fracturing of my parents' hopes and dreams, and in many ways the promise of America." The family fell into hardship with their breadwinner not able to work.

Howard worked menial jobs to support his family as soon as he was able to. Again, in his own words: "As the oldest of three children, I had to grow up quickly. I started earning money at an early age. At twelve, I had a paper route; later I worked behind the counter at the local luncheonette. At sixteen, I got an after-school job in the garment district of Manhattan, at a furrier, stretching animal skins. It was horrendous work and left thick callouses on my thumbs. I spent one hot summer in a sweatshop, steaming yarn at a knitting factory. I always gave part of my earnings to my mother—not because she insisted but because I felt bad for the position my parents were in."

"I always wanted to do something to make a difference." Howard learned early on the struggle that low-income families have to go through when they are squeezed out of jobs and out of health care. As CEO of a company employing many from the low-income bracket, he can empathize with his employees' life situations. He thus early on instituted a wide range of perks, benefits, and assistance called Your Special Blend at Starbucks for all employees who work twenty or more hours a week.

Howard has been quoted for saying, "service is a lost art in America. It's not viewed as a professional job to work behind a counter. We don't believe that. We want to provide our people with dignity and self-esteem, so we offer tangible benefits." These benefits include bonuses, 401(k) matching, discounted stock purchase options, adoption assistance, and complete health coverage for full- and part-time employees and their dependents, including domestic partners. Further, the company runs a college plan that reimburses college fees for courses completed with the Arizona State University's online program.

Howard Schultz shows true empathy for his employees because he has been in their shoes. He has lived their pain. He has shed their tears. Some see the benefits the company offers as extra costs. Mr. Schultz sees them as moral incentives that keep baristas happy who in turn keep customers happy.

8. MARY BARA, GENERAL MOTORS

In March 2010, twenty-nine-year-old Brooke Melton was doing 58 mph in her white 2005 Chevrolet Cobalt in a 55-mph zone when the car suddenly stalled. The engine shut off. The power steering turned off. The airbag was disabled.

The Chevy spun out of control, hydroplaned, collided with another car, veered off the road, and crashed into a deep creek. Brooke was killed in the accident. The Police ruled that she was driving too fast in the rainy conditions. Brooke's parents who knew of their daughter's safe driving habits were not convinced that a mere 3 mph speed over the limit was the cause of their daughter's death. Her dad said, "I knew in my heart and in my gut there was something wrong with the car, that it wasn't her fault."

Mary Barra took the helm of the third-largest carmaker in the world in the midst of the worst crisis the company ever faced in its century-old history. In February 2014, General Motors acknowledged that a faulty ignition switch was responsible for the crash that caused several cars to crash and people to lose their lives. The company first recalled 800,000 vehicles and said they were aware of a dozen deaths. Soon, however, the problem would grow beyond anybody's imagination and General Motors would end up recalling 12.8 million cars.

The faulty ignition switch would be linked to 124 deaths! An investigation into the company revealed that employees had known of the defect for a period going back ten years before Brooke Melton's death. GM's engineers held meetings in as early as 2005 to discuss the issue. Mary Barra as the new CEO had one single question to answer to families of the victims and a congressional panel who called her to Washington DC to testify: why did GM knowingly sell cars that were killing people?

Faced with such a huge crisis, some CEOs retract into a defensive posture. They play on words to deflect responsibility. They focus on saving the company from expenses and liabilities and often on saving their own jobs. Ms. Barra did the opposite. She took responsibility for the problem and acknowledged that there was indeed an issue and a "pattern of incompetence and neglect" going back years.

She apologized repeatedly to the families of the victims without mincing words saying, "I am deeply sorry." She hired famed mass-injury attorney Kenneth Feinberg as a consultant showing that she was being genuine in caring for the victims' well-being. She immediately appointed a new vice president of Global Vehicle Safety to ensure current car models are safer. And she initiated a series of measures internally to get to the root causes of the problem. The Wall Street Journal praised her for not arguing that these were "the problems of a company that no longer exists and a product that's no longer made." In the end, GM paid $600 million in compensation to surviving victims and forfeited $900 million to the United States. Ms. Barra commented, "… whatever mistakes were made in the past, we will not shirk from our responsibilities now and in the future. Today's GM will do the right thing."

9. ANDY GROVE, INTEL

The late Andy Grove is often remembered for his paranoia – his insistence that every leader needs to be constantly looking over her shoulder. Grove, the legendary CEO of Intel, wrote a best seller titled "Only the Paranoid Survive" and he is credited for making the phrase popular as an idiom that is nowadays casually used everywhere by management who wants to look cool. Grove wrote about rapid changes in our environment that many times catch us by surprise. These shifts can be the result of almost anything – a change in law, the emergence of a competitor, evolution of technology, etc. Grove calls these moments Strategic Inflection Point and he argues that only if we are paranoid about them can we survive them. However, what many people do not talk about Andy

Grove is his deep sense of humility that I believe was as important to him navigating the Strategic Inflection Points as him being paranoid.

Andy Grove was born in a Jewish family in Budapest, Hungary. When he was a young boy, the Second World War broke and hundreds of thousands of Hungarian Jews were sent to concentration camps. His father was among these prisoners. Grove and his mother hid their identities and were sheltered by a Christian family. After the war, he was reunited with his father but had to live through the tumultuous post war years in Hungary. By the time he was 20, Grove escaped to the United States. He arrived penniless and barely able to speak any English. Grove would, however, epitomize the idea of the American Dream. He started work as a busboy and made his way to college. By 1963, he graduated with a Ph.D. in chemical engineering from the University of California, Berkeley. This life experience of Grove would inculcate a deep sense of humility in him.

Grove believed in simplicity. He famously maintained a cubicle office at Intel. He did not believe in the concept of closed mahogany-lined offices in an ivory tower. He pushed a culture where employees could just walk to him with questions. And when questioned he never assumed that he had the better answer. He encouraged constructive criticism and decisions arrived at through active brainstorming. He maintained a flat organization and nobody received any privilege. Intel had no designated parking spots for their executives. One day, Andy Grove arrived a few minutes late for a meeting – he could not find an available spot to park and was driving around looking for one in the parking lot! Grove deeply respected other people's ideas and that manifested in his deep sense of humility.

10. JEN HSUN HUANG, NVIDIA

In 2015, the Harvard Business Review named Jen Hsun Huang one of the world's one hundred best-performing CEOs over the lifetime of their tenure. As I am writing on him now in December 2017, I am running to keep updating this chapter to keep up with the news! He has been nominated or recognized by many major publications, including Fortune, as the Businessman of the Year! He is truly a rainmaker.

The Taiwan-born Huang has been a hard worker who learned from every one of his experiences from his early childhood years. To Jen Hsun, life is learning. Jen Hsun came to the United States as a young child. His uncle and aunt registered him with the Oneida Baptist Church reform school in Kentucky. There, he scrubbed toilets for chores. As a teenager, he picked up on table tennis and by the age of fifteen he placed third in junior table doubles at the U.S. Open. He appeared in the pages of Sports Illustrated.

Jen Hsun graduated from Oregon State University with a degree in electrical engineering and later received his Master's degree from Stanford. By the age of thirty, he founded NVIDIA with two friends. Today, Jen Hsun, whose name graces one of the engineering buildings in Stanford, is one of the most admired CEOs in Silicon Valley.

Jen Hsun does not see hardships or failures as showstoppers but rather as learning points in an ever-evolving career. He readily admits that he has made plenty of mistakes in his career. However, he views these mistakes as teaching moments. He recollects how as a young twenty-four-year-old manager he felt possessive about his team. But he later realized that teams are fluid and a good leader is happy both when people join the team and when people leave the team.

Jen Hsun and NVIDIA have been leading the Virtual Reality space with cutting-edge innovations. While the whole world is hyping this technology, Jen Hsun cautioned that we are still twenty years away from experiencing a truly satisfying VR experience. Jen Hsun is a rare leader who can admit the true level of maturity of a technology that the media is clamoring to hear about. He learned early on that creating perceptions without a factual basis is not leadership.

He also learned how to pivot after mistakes. Several years ago, his company decided to invest heavily in expanding their chip AI capabilities, and Nvidia is now producing GPUs (graphics processing units) that can quickly handle complex AI jobs. While many chip producers are facing declining sales, Nvidia is surging ahead and finding new chip applications in healthcare. Valuation of the company has now almost reached around 150 billion dollars. I remain very optimistic that we will hear more about this leader in the many years ahead. And many analysts project that NVIDIA could be the next Intel of the industry.

I have been observing Jen Hsun Huang since 1997 and have become one of his fans. When I was planning this chapter, my top ten irreplaceable CEOs, Jen Hsun immediately came to my mind and I had a place for him on this list. He is a great fighter and diehard guy. So far, he has not disappointed his fans and seems to have never ending pleasant surprises for the industry.

Just reading the stories here, we see many similarities and patterns. Great CEOs exhibit personal traits that set them apart. We all to some extent have these—enthusiasm, determination, re-invention, persistence, humility, instinctive, empathic, pioneering, responsible, and having a love of learning—but great leaders radiate these traits. Beyond this, what has also caught my attention and curiosity is the disproportionate number of India-born CEOs in the largest companies in the world. Besides Indra Nooyi in my list above, we see the brilliant performance from Sundar Pichai of Google, Satya Nadella of Microsoft, Shantanu Narayen of Adobe, and many many more. It makes me wonder about the education or environment that makes cultivates management talent.

Great CEOs also pick leaders with these traits to work for them and to succeed them. It is necessary but not sufficient for a leader to have these traits. They also need to ensure that their team develop these traits. A leader is always thinking about tomorrow and a great tomorrow is prepared by picking the team and successors who exhibit these leadership traits.

In the coming years, I am hoping two other CEOs in my circle of acquaintances will extend this list: Don Jin (DJ) Koh CEO of Samsung Mobile and Stein Kruse CEO of the Holland America Group.

DJ Koh, Head of Samsung Electronics Mobile group, stands out as a leader who is always heedful of advice. Many executives talk to their mentors like many teenagers talk to their counselors—they hardly pay attention. DJ is certainly not like these executives. He humbly welcomes ideas, feedback, and criticisms with the conviction that these are meant for his own improvement. He also learns from past mistakes. During the Note 7 fiasco where the device was bursting into flames in places all over the world due to faulty batteries, and losing the company billions of dollars, he remained steady and patient. (Imagine how unpleasant it must be to be asked to turn off your phone on a flight in case of explosion, if you are the CEO of that phone company!) He spent time listening to customers, critics—with severe, humiliating things to say—employees, and advisors. He reflected deeply. He was patient and came up with clear and decisive solutions and led Samsung to a great comeback. DJ spared no expense and implemented company-wide improvements to regain the customers' trust. In a corporate culture where the CEO is often seen as a demigod, DJ is an exception.

Stein Kruse calls himself The Chief Worrier. Holland America, founded in 1873, traces its roots all the way back to the Netherlands and is now based in Seattle. It is one of the most recognizable name brands in the cruise industry offering an unsurpassed experience in luxury on the seas. Stein leads Holland America like the captain at the helm of one of his cruise ships: with passion and knowledge, but most importantly, with a laser sharp focus in improving the experience and safety of the passengers.

Besides these favorite top 10 CEOs that I picked, I am sure many of you would pick yours too as we are living in a world of transformation and technologies are changing even faster than ever. I believe everyone should have their own favourite CEOs to learn from and model. Elon Musk is a revolutionary entrepreneur with big ambitions, though I feel he has spread his effort across too many initiatives, not focusing on one at a time. I certainly hope I'm wrong and wish he will able to keep the momentum going in all of them.

In future, I am hopeful we will be watching many more new superstars rise and fall. What I'd like to emphasize is that those who will be taking over the world are willing to build from scratch. They must realize that if there were no previous pioneers who set the frame, there would be no playground   today.

CHAPTER 12: AM I READY FOR TOMORROW?

"People can move mountains yet cannot change their habits; they can bury the ocean yet cannot fill their desires."
Old Chinese proverb

"Let us never know what old age is. Let us know the happiness time brings, not count the years."
Decimius Ausonius, Roman Poet

"Old age, believe me, is a good and pleasant thing. It is true you are gently shouldered off the stage, but then you are given such a comfortable front stall as spectator."
Confucius

"I will never be an old man. To me, old age is always fifteen years older than I am."
Francis Bacon

"Made weak by time and fate, but strong in will / To strive, to seek, to find and not to yield."
"Ulysses", Alfred Lord Tennyson

Finish Planting the Tree

I often say to executives that a successful CEO tends to complete the deadline for tomorrow's work today, not push today's work for tomorrow. I started my first book, *Wonder*, by posing an extraordinary question: "why die?" I reflected on the fact that companies should not have an expiration date. Unlike tangible or natural objects, a company is first and foremost a set of ideas that can be refreshed to match the new demands of its environment. Hence, theoretically a company does not need to die.

I argued then that Customer Experience is the barometer that measures a changing environment. And, if a company constantly optimizes its solutions and offerings using this measure from its customers, it can always stay relevant and can avert dying. I wish I could propose a similar formula for all of us mortals!

Growing old and passing the baton to the younger generation is in fact what keep us humans alive. The single purpose of our existence, biologists tell us, is to propagate our genes and not to hold on to them forever. Holding on to a fixed genome in a changing environment is like a company selling buggy whips to Tesla owners. Before the internet exploded in popularity, no one could have thought of the life we are enjoying right now, much less to talk of iPhones, smart TVs and the idea of staying connected and working from anywhere in the world. Today, we hear talk of terms like bitcoin, blockchain and the internet of everything. We are living in exciting times and who knows what else the future holds for us?

Companies evolve by adapting their ideas. Living organisms evolve by passing their genes to a more adaptable generation. In other words, for us humans, the question is not "why die?" but rather "why not die?"

In an old story from the Middle East, we are told of a farmer who is planting a seedling in dirt when suddenly the end of the world comes upon him. Dark clouds appear, the ground shakes, animals panic and belch, birds take flight and flee in vain. The wise farmer, the story goes, is the one who finishes planting the tree as everything around him collapses. The wisdom of this tale is that even in the eventuality of our own demise and the demise of everything around us, we should remain focused. We don't have to worry about things changing. They will. And we should look forward to the changes and embrace them.

What I Saw in China in Year 2000

Back in the early part of 2000s, I was traveling in China when China was just getting started in the venture startup eruption. Early one morning I went to a famous bookstore in the New World Town Complex in Beijing. There were not many people out yet and the store was quiet. I wondered over to their small business section and was absolutely shocked! There was literally no one elsewhere in the bookstore, but this one section—the business section and government workers section—was crowded with young street beggars. All of them were so focused on reading the books they didn't notice there was a stranger there watching them. I had never seen people with such a laser-like focus. I guessed that they had come from far away provinces to the big city to follow their dream. They had nothing and didn't look like much, but I saw something else. They reminded me of the time when I was chasing my own dream during my childhood and I saw the future of China right there. That was the buildup phase of what was going to lead to a great boom. I thought the future of China becoming a world leader was not too far away, even though many people, even some of my friends that led the top businesses in the world, laughed at me when I said that. It was the hunger that I saw in the eyes of these young people that gave me a glimpse of that brewing potential energy.

I started as a young man in a post-war country, without a job, and with only small dreams. It would have been easy to stay stuck in a thought pattern that was limited, depressed, or frustrated. How did I train my mind to stay optimistic and keep focused on my future?

I devoured any story I could find on men who started their lives in abject poverty and made it big. I have discussed several examples in this book and in my previous book. Chung Ju-yung, founder of Hyundai, was the son of impoverished peasants.

Andy Grove of Intel escaped the Nazis, surviving the holocaust. Steve Jobs, founder of Apple, grew up in foster care. President Barack Obama had an absent father whom he barely knew. The world is replete with examples of businessmen and businesswomen, athletes, politicians and leaders who started their lives in situations worse than our own situations.

Sometimes, the deeper we are in our own predicaments, the stronger our desire to achieve and the higher our ultimate reach is. The further back the elastic band of life pulls us, the further forward we are catapulted once the holding force lets go. Convince your mind that if the role models could make it then you too can make it. Study their examples. Learn their lessons. Derive convictions from their struggles. Then keep your mind busy looking   at   your   tomorrows!

In the Year 2525

In 1968, the pop-rock duo Zager and Evans recorded the hit song "In the Year 2525." The song shot to number one on the Billboard Hot 100 for six weeks in 1969. It peaked at number one in the UK Singles Chart for three weeks that same year. The song, which starts with the verse "In the year 2525 / If man is still alive / If woman can survive / They may find..." invites listeners to dream of what humanity would look like in the far future. Many around the world including me were mesmerized by Zager and Evans' lyrics and tunes. The song went on to be covered at least sixty times in seven languages.

The popularity of Zager and Evans' song shows our collective fascination with the future. The writers referenced the year 2525 and then 3535, 4545, etc. in the song because of its rhyming cadence, not because they really intended to predict the future in those exact years. It is impossible to predict the distant future and nearly impossible to predict even the near future. There are just too many variables at play in deciding what's next.

When the interdependence of more than a handful of variables influences an outcome, the ability to predict that outcome is exponentially more complex. Stephen Hawking, the famed physicist, famously said, "One can't predict the weather more than a few days in advance." The probability that it will either rain or shine next week is incredibly difficult to predict because of the many variables influencing the weather.

I have found an interesting shift in the most valuable companies in America over 100 years by comparing the 1917, 1967, and 2017 top 10 list from Forbes. As you can see from the 2017 list, the top six are from the tech sector and none of those were big names or big industries in the past. Oil and construction-related are not even on the list anymore. It is extremely hard to forecast what will happen in the next fifty years.

Here are the Top 10 for 2017 (company name and market cap in US dollars): Apple 898B / Alphabet 719B/ Microsoft 644B / Amazon 543B / Facebook 518B / Berkshire Hathaway 452B / Johnson & Johnson 374B / Exxon Mobile 350B/ JP Morgan Chase 340B / Bank of American 286B

Now look back at the Top 10 for 1967: IBM 258B / AT&T 200B / Eastman Kodak 117B / General Motors 171B / Standard Oil 106 B / Texaco 82B / Sears 64 B / General Electric 63B / Polaroid 58B / Gulf Oil 58B

And go back a little further to the Top 10 from 1917: US Steel 46B / AT&T 14B / Standard Oil 10.7 B / Bethlehem Steel 7.1B / Swift & Co. 5.7B / International Harvester 4.9B / DuPont 4.9B / Midvale Steel 4.8B / US Rubber 4.6B.

What changed in America so dramatically and why couldn't these leading executives stay more relevant? 1917 was the Industrialist Era. In 1911, both John D. Rockefeller's Standard Oil and J.P. Morgan's U.S. Steel were facing antitrust action. Standard Oil, which controlled over 90% of all oil in the United States by 1900, got split up into thirty-four independent companies after a ruling by the Supreme Court. However, U.S. Steel, which controlled 67% of steel in the country, was able to weather the antitrust storm at the time. U.S. Steel – which was considered the world's first "billion dollars" company – reigned supreme in the U.S. based on the value of its assets. Meanwhile, Standard Oil of N.J. (a fragment of the Standard Oil breakup) was still able to finish in the third spot on the list.

Fast forward fifty years, and oil is still big. Standard Oil of N.J. (eventually to be renamed Exxon Corp. in 1972) was the fifth biggest company in the country. Texaco and Gulf Oil, both of which later merged into Chevron (another Standard Oil offshoot) also make the top 10 in terms of market valuation. But the economy was changing. By 1967 we were entering the Hardware Era.

Aside from energy, the 1967 list seems dominated by companies that make tangible things. IBM was making some of the first and most advanced computers, GM was the largest U.S. auto manufacturer, and both Kodak and Polaroid made cameras. General Electric, a conglomerate, made everything from computers to jet engines at this time.

Fast forward to now, and companies like Facebook, Amazon, Google, Microsoft, and Apple have taken over. We can call 2017 the Platform Era. These five companies make billions and Facebook and Google are able to dominate global ad revenues through scale. Meanwhile, many of the leaders from 1967 have fallen: Polaroid, Kodak, and Sears Canada filed for bankruptcy. And of the big names from 1917, only AT&T remains of significance.

This picture gets more complicated if we shift our perspective internationally. Take China as an example. Baidu, Alibaba and Tencent were not in existence in 1967 and in 2017 they were massive forces propelling China into a future where it is not simply redefining itself but redefining the whole world. In the fourth quarter of 2017, Tencent was the sixth largest company worldwide and Alibaba the eighth largest company worldwide by market cap. Only a few years ago, it would have been inconceivable to imagine a Chinese company eclipsing names like Facebook and JP Morgan Chase. What is even more amazing is that these Chinese companies are not slowing down anytime soon. They are, in many people's eyes, just getting started!

There are 16,500 companies being created in China daily or 6 million companies created in 2017. Take a minute and let these numbers sink in. How many Baidu, Alibaba and Tencent do we have in this mix? How many will place their names on the top 10 companies billboard in 2027? How many of them will create products that we will not be able to live without? These questions are mind-boggling.

This raises the ultimate question: what will the next fifty years hold – and how many names from 2017 will remain? There's no way anyone can predict the future about which companies will be thriving then. Nowadays, the FAANG (Facebook, Amazon, Apple, Netflix, Google) are top of mind for most investors. But, if I would pick or bet on a company today, perhaps companies in the consumer hardware and social media sector wouldn't be my favorite. The landscape of technology has been changing much faster especially after the digital era merged into the Internet phenomena in the last decade. So I would bet that software-based core technologies and life sciences will be the most promising industries to watch.

In 2013, the U.S. Department of Labor reported that sixty-five percent of today's schoolchildren will eventually be employed in jobs that have yet to be created! Yes, that is correct—most of our children will be working to build products and solutions that do not exist today! Look at the phenomenal transformation of the last centennial or even last ten years of revolution in technology and changing of lifestyle. Who would have thought we would be living in the world of the Internet, a digital era?

Your next best tool, besides having a crystal ball, is having the ability to create your own future instead of worrying about it. I certainly don't claim that I have a crystal ball that allows me to clearly know what will happen in a few years or in a few decades. Rather, I think vision about our biggest challenges and curiosity about our core needs might give us valuable clues.

In my journey thus far, many people have helped me to become the man that I am and I am grateful to them in so many ways. And of all the good that has come from achieving my goals, my greatest reward is to see many people inspired to start their own journey, to begin their own path. That gives me such hope for the world.

Therefore, in this next phase of my life, I will be working to share my experiences with my mentees, and students and close friends, so that they too can become successful in their own way and do good for society and the world, to create a lot of jobs and spend their time and money in a way that is good for the world. Success to me now means that my legacy never dies and my learning keeps moving on to the world of delivering dreams, their own personal dreams. After meeting so many people and helping so many students, there were many times I have been reminded of myself in their hungry and sparkling eyes. I see myself in their eyes. What I hope to achieve, is that the next time they see themselves in the eyes of another, they can carry on my legacy and help more to succeed, paying forward what I have received from those who have supported me along the way.

The poet Khalil Gibran once said, "Yesterday is but today's memory, and tomorrow is today's dream." In this book, I have attempted to demonstrate that while the ink of yesterday has dried, the pen of tomorrow is still between our fingers. Our tomorrow is ours to dream. Our tomorrow is ours to write. Do not for once believe you cannot reinvent your tomorrow. And, do not let anyone write your tomorrow. This is the essence of this book. As I chart my own journey and my own tomorrow, I wish all of you a most bright TOMORROW. Good luck!

75152979R00089

Made in the USA
San Bernardino, CA
25 April 2018